# The Londoner and his library

Brian Groombridge
Research Director
Research Institute for Consumer Affairs

The Research Institute for Consumer Affairs

Designed by Harold Bartram
Printed by the Shenval Press

# Contents

# List of tables

# Acknowledgements

*The Londoner and his library* is the first research report to be published by RICA. The work on which it is based was supported by a grant from the Library Association, to which body RICA owes especial thanks. RICA wishes also to acknowledge the sustained interest of the Association of Metropolitan Chief Librarians, and advice, information and help received from the BBC's Audience Research Department, the Consumers' Association, the Institute of Community Studies, the Institute of Municipal Treasurers, and the National Institute of Adult Education.

I would like personally to thank the many people who helped on the project, especially the Chief Librarians in the boroughs surveyed, and the anonymous members of the public who were willing to answer the questions. The borough librarians – R. P. Bateman, E. V. Corbett, C. Edwards, W. R. Maidment, R. D. Rates, R. Rouse and Herbert Ward – encouraged the enquiry in every way possible and the report has greatly benefited from the candour and objectivity with which they commented on it in draft. I am also grateful to eight other librarians for direct help in various forms – the late Hilda Jennings, Daphne Grose, F. A. Hatt, L. Hasker, R. Helliwell, K. A. Mallaber, Neil Rhind and P. W. Plumb – and, though this acknowledgement will surprise him, to a distinguished past-President of the Library Association, Edward Sydney, for inspiration on the subject long before the research was contemplated. I owe a considerable editorial debt to Edward Hutchinson, to my Consumers' Association colleagues Eirlys Roberts and Alastair Macgeorge, and to RICA's Trustees. Dr W. Belson gave valuable advice about the Index mentioned in Chapter 5, and Alderman J. C. Lawder about a library committee's point of view.

It is not possible fully to convey the extent to which such an enquiry and the report upon it are a collaborative effort, but they could not have been achieved without Jillian MacGuire (who designed the sample, acted as statistical adviser and contributed material for the book in draft), Jennifer Owen (who organised the fieldworkers on whose accuracy and 'ear' so much of the report depends), Joy Samuel (who acted as research assistant in the first stages and editorial consultant throughout), and the staff of RICA (whose hard work and enthusiasm have gone far beyond the mere fulfilment of contract).

Brian Groombridge
April 1964

Chapter 1

# Introduction: scope and purpose of this report

It is now (1964) seven years since the Roberts Committee on Public Libraries was set up, and five since it reported.* Since then two Working Parties have also reported, making specific recommendations about standards and about inter-library co-operation, and in the light of these reports the Government has introduced legislation which will for the first time lay upon public library authorities the statutory duty to provide an efficient service.† The three official reports were the work of experts – professional librarians, local government officers, councillors and others closely concerned with the service. To examine such technical matters is clearly no job for laymen.

This report deals with a complementary theme: the public for which the public library service is provided. It does this in two ways – by giving information about the nature of that public, as it is at present made up, and by reporting what people say about public libraries, not only those who are members, but also those who used to belong and those who never have. Its closest relatives in British writing on this subject are, therefore, Mass Observation's now dated *Reading in Tottenham* (1947)‡ and the Society of Young Publishers' Survey *Books in London, 1959*.|| It is more comprehensive in scope and more detailed in its analysis than the Tottenham survey, while it goes in some depth into issues that necessarily played only a small part in *Books in London*.

This report rests on four main assumptions. The first is that, although the official reports have rightly concentrated attention on the standards that should be achieved by an efficient service, there is a tendency to lose

* *The Structure of the Public Library Service in England and Wales:* Report of the Committee appointed by the Minister of Education in September 1957. HMSO, 1959 (Cmnd. 660).

† *Standards of Public Library Service in England and Wales*. HMSO, 1962. *Inter-Library Co-operation in England and Wales*. HMSO, 1962.

‡ *Reading in Tottenham*, Borough of Tottenham, Libraries and Museum Department, 1947.

|| 'Books in London, 1959', in *Books*, the journal of the National Book League, January–February 1960, pp. 7–22.

sight of that very public in whose name these and other current recommendations for reform are being made. For what kinds of people are public libraries provided? This question needs to be answered if the service is to be not only approved by the professional, but also welcomed and used by the layman who supplies the entire enterprise with its purpose.

The survey on which this report is based would not have been undertaken at all without the prior judgment that the public library service is of importance to the community. Given the importance of the service – the second assumption – it is necessary to assess whether library authorities are catering for as many people as they could, as well as they might. It is not assumed, however, that everyone *ought* to belong to a public library, nor yet that librarians must consider themselves failures if there are minorities who persist in not being enrolled.

The third assumption is that just as the future structure of the service is a matter not only for experts, but also for the general public, so is the matter of whether the service is working in practice as well as it should. Obviously librarians ought, in a sense, to be better judges and critics of libraries than laymen; their professionalism would not amount to much if they were not. And yet because of their professionalism it is difficult for librarians to look at libraries with the eye of the library user. It is assumed, accordingly, that no further justification is required for finding out what the people who pay for the service actually think about it.

The last assumption is that librarians are more likely to fulfil their ambition to make their libraries reach more people more effectively if they are guided by knowledge, and not only by opinion or partial observation, about the nature of the public that they are serving or failing to serve. Librarians have a strong sense of public service and, as the deliberations at the annual conferences of the Library Association show, they are capable of criticising themselves with a harshness rarely equalled by outsiders, excepting perhaps Sir Alan Herbert. Yet self-criticism may be damaging if it is not founded on knowledge. Two typically self-critical speeches well illustrate the need and also provide several relevant hypotheses to be checked by the findings in this report – an address by A. H. Bill to the 1962 conference of the Library Association,* and another by D. E. Gerard at a weekend conference of the London and Home Counties Branch of the Association in the same year.†

Mr Bill, speaking as the Honorary Treasurer of the Association of

* *Proceedings* of the Annual Conference of the Library Association, 1962, pp. 62–70.

† *Book Provision for Special Needs*. The Library Association, London and Home Counties Branch, 1962, pp. 15–30.

Assistant Librarians, provided what one delegate described as that association's traditional 'stick of ginger'. It was part of his intention 'to discuss the failure of the public library service to find its proper place in the community and the reasons for this failure', a charge which he justified in these words:

> What impact *does* the public library service make then? . . . Superficially, a considerable one. Larger bookfunds (and in the last few years many new buildings) have brought increased issues, and in some places up to 40 per cent of the population are registered as members: it is easy to be persuaded that the community is making good use of an adequate service.

But a closer look at records of membership and use would, he feared, reveal a less satisfactory picture:

> The number of people actually *using* the library at any time is only about half of those registered – at the most about one in five of the population, and in many areas a much lower proportion even than this. This fact is one which we constantly conceal or obscure by our use of grossly inflated and unrealistic statistics of 'registered readers'.

Furthermore, the turnover of members is disquieting:

> The turnover . . . is very high – far higher than can be accounted for by population movements and other natural causes. The scale of turnover is such that most people must be – however transiently – registered members of a public library. The conclusion is inescapable: most let their membership lapse because they do not find what they want.

Who are our readers? This is a question that worries some of the radical spirits in the profession, of whom D. E. Gerard is evidently one. He claimed that a young librarian entering the profession would notice that:

> Not all the classes in society use us. . . . He will see that when we talk about the public, we really mean a narrow band taken from somewhere in the middle of the middle class. He may even ask why doesn't it grow any wider, or why don't women use the reference library?

Mr Gerard, who is the Deputy Chief Librarian for Nottingham, invited his colleagues to:

> Stuff cotton wool in your ears if you do not like the term 'working class' (because) in regaining our purpose, our direction, socially speaking, must take us downwards to the 80 per cent for whom no breakthrough has yet been achieved. It is no use our civilised design for living which, as librarians, is what we stand for, being confined everlastingly to this self-conscious minority.

One may observe, in passing, that this attitude may not be as 'progressive' as it sounds. Presumably even a narrow middle band of the middle class is entitled to make use of public libraries, and concern about the working class, like concern about youth, can easily carry with it the implication that the workers are more in need of cultural salvation than any other group in society. It is a fashionable, but dubious, proposition. However, the issue raised by Mr Gerard and other dissatisfied librarians is important, and one better served by facts about the social composition of the library public than by speculations.

Collecting the facts is, of course, normally a piecemeal and limited process. The facts about 'The Londoner' of the title were discovered from a sample of over 1,300 adult Londoners, and the core of the report is about a representative 500 of them. The exposition follows this course: first, the places in which the survey was carried out are briefly described and the composition of their populations discussed (Chapter 2). After considering the official accounts of the extent to which the people in these places are users of their public libraries, the detailed analysis begins (Chapter 3). The nature of the public is examined and the characteristics of members isolated (Chapters 4 and 5). What people said about libraries and about their reasons for being or not being members is reported in Chapters 6, 7 and 8. The report concludes with a commentary about the role of public libraries, inspired by what has been discovered about their actual and potential membership.

# Chapter 2

# Places, people and libraries

In this report, 'the public' is represented by a sample of the resident adult population in seven London boroughs, interviewed in October to December 1962. The seven boroughs were chosen to represent the metropolis as a whole, not the capital at its wealthiest. They are Chelsea, Finsbury, Hampstead, Lewisham, Stepney, Stoke Newington and Wandsworth. Before the creation of Greater London, they constituted one in four of the London boroughs; they are geographically dispersed and socially dissimilar, they vary enormously in size and population, and considerably in the size of their library rate. By one of the most familiar criteria – the proportion of the population in library membership – they also differ in the extent of their success.

## The places

It is unnecessary to describe these seven boroughs in detail because they are meant only to stand for the totality of varied communities that make up metropolitan London, and, in any case, when the enquiry was conducted the boroughs concerned were already within sight of supersession by the new administrative areas of Greater London.* Furthermore, the daily mobility of London's population, together with the existence of co-operative schemes which embrace the separate metropolitan library authorities, would make it misleading to concentrate too closely on these particular areas. Nevertheless, they are the places where the interviews were conducted and the libraries in those areas were the ones to which most of the library members interviewed currently belonged.

**Chelsea** is a small, compact borough (660 acres) with a population of 48,550.† It lies just west of Westminster, between the River Thames and

* At the time of publication, the Greater London Council was being set up alongside the borough authorities. The descriptions in this chapter applied at the time of the survey.

† The population figures in this section are taken from statistics issued by the Association of Metropolitan Chief Librarians.

Kensington, with which it is to be merged under the Greater London Plan. Its popular image is not too far from the reality – it is a fashionable, artistic quarter, famous for its Flower Shows and its Pensioners, for the historical associations of Cheyne Walk, the Royal Court Theatre, Peter Jones' store and Lots Road Power Station.

Unlike the other boroughs, it has only one library building, conveniently situated in the centre of the borough, and easily accessible from all parts. The library was the first in London to provide separate rooms for children and the building also houses a reference library, lending library, newspaper and magazine rooms and a small gallery for displaying pictures and prints of local interest. One of the ways in which the metropolitan boroughs collaborate is by buying, between them, all non-fiction books that are published in Britain, each library specialising in certain subjects. Chelsea carries the Special Collections on Costume, Botany and Palaeontology.* In March 1963, the library stocked over 126,000 volumes, available between 9 am and 8 pm on weekdays, or between 9 am and 5 pm on Saturdays. There were also over 1,200 gramophone records (a collection started in 1960).†

**Finsbury** (population 33,020) is even smaller (587 acres) than Chelsea and due for incorporation with its northern neighbour, Islington. In appearance and atmosphere it is the antithesis of Chelsea, with hundreds of tenement houses due for demolition, small manufacturing firms bringing in a large daytime population, commercial warehouses, and heavy traffic. It is, in a sense, the wealthy City of London's backyard, but it is also the home of Sadler's Wells and a College of Advanced Technology. Though the area is small, the borough is cut through by main roads into the City, but no part of the borough is beyond fifteen minutes' or so walk from any other part.

Finsbury has three library buildings: an old central library, a newly opened branch library (1962), and a separately housed children's department (Treasure Island) in which children are encouraged to do their homework and learn recreative crafts. The Central Library has adult lending and reference departments and a gramophone record collection. In 1963 the service had over 111,000 books and almost 1,800 records available, as in

* There are also special collections of books in foreign languages, e.g. in Danish at Chelsea and Hebrew at Stepney, and the libraries house between them a Joint Fiction Reserve.

† A table showing comparative particulars for all seven boroughs, together with their library rates, is given in Appendix 1, p. 103.

Chelsea, between 9 am and 8 pm (5 pm on Saturdays). The Metropolitan Special Collection at Finsbury is on Photography.

**Hampstead** (to be part of the new Camden borough with Holborn and St Pancras) covers 2,266 acres and has a population of 98,240. Its popular reputation is as well defined as Chelsea's, and again largely justified. It looks solid and prosperous, it is bracingly sited on the hills to the north-west; it is relatively well populated with millionaires, intellectuals and executives. It has its artistic quarters, its streets of bed-sitters, and its cafés are much frequented by *au pair* girls and students. But not all of its 2,266 acres are fashionable or cosmopolitan. 'Lived here' plaques are not conspicuous in the streets of Kilburn, in the west of the borough. Like Finsbury, Hampstead is cut through by main arterial roads into the centre of London, which divide the borough into four long, thin sections, with public transport running only north and south. It supports five library buildings – one central and four branches serving each of these sections.

The Central Library houses a gramophone record collection (over 8,000 discs in 1963) and a reference library that is much used by students. In all, Hampstead libraries had a bookstock of 238,000 volumes in 1963. On two nights of the week the libraries are open until 8 pm, and on the other three until 7 pm. Its Special Collection is Philosophy and Psychology.

**Lewisham** (population 222,170; 7,017 acres) is a sprawling area to the south-east of London, bordering on Kent. It embraces thirteen separate districts, all of which have more or less individuality of their own. The riverside borough of Deptford is to be combined with it in the Greater London amalgamations. It is primarily a residential area from which many people travel each day to work in the City (there are sixteen Southern Region railway stations within its borders). Administration of the local government services is centralised in Catford, but there is a lack of cohesion, partly brought about, or at any rate exacerbated, by inadequate public transport across the borough from east to west.

The library system in Lewisham to some extent reflects these difficulties. One building, roughly in the centre of the borough, has since 1901 been designated the Central Library and there were ten branch libraries, supported by a mobile library visiting four sites (now five), when the survey was carried out. Half the main reference library and the gramophone record library are at the central building, the rest of the reference library being at the Bromley Road branch (opened since the survey). Apart from the mobile library (which shuts earlier) and a local history department at Manor House (which closes at 6 pm on some evenings) the usual opening hours are 10 am until 7.30 pm (6 pm on Saturdays). In 1963, Lewisham libraries had an available stock of 367,000 books (including the Special Collection of books about the British Isles) and nearly 14,000 gramophone records (two branch collections of gramophone records have since been started).

**Stepney** (population 90,480), to be combined with Bethnal Green and Poplar to make Tower Hamlets, consists of 1,770 acres; more people have visited it than usually realise – to see the Tower of London. It is 'East End' and 'Dockland', Whitechapel and Cable Street. It was badly bombed but, behind the scarred façades, new local authority estates of flats are going up. They are surrounded by wharves, clothing factories, paint firms, breweries and the blackened offices of Leman Street. Amidst a great deal of ugliness there are unexpected beauties – the Royal Foundation of St Katherine, and churches by Nicholas Hawksmoor.

Stepney has six library buildings – ample accommodation, some of it old and most of it now in the wrong place. Boundary changes have left some of these buildings on the periphery of the borough, and new building plans have isolated four of them – one in the middle of Queen Mary College (University of London), two flanked by warehouses, and the fourth on the wrong side of a road through to the docks, about half a mile from a residential estate. The Stepney libraries carry a stock of 166,000 books and 5,200 gramophone records (1963 figures), and these are available between 10 am and 8 pm (5 pm on Wednesdays and Saturdays). Reference libraries and newsrooms (all but two branches have the latter) open an hour earlier. The London Special Collections on General and American Literature are maintained in Stepney.

**Stoke Newington** is a fairly small and compact borough (population 52,180; 863 acres). By the Greater London Plan it is to become part of the enlarged Hackney, together with Shoreditch. It is mainly residential, and has changed its character rapidly since the war. The London County Council Woodberry Down Estate has taken the place of Victorian mansions; skilled workers have succeeded wealthy business men. It is no longer the village-like retreat, handy for the City, that it once was, but the official *Guide's* boast 'This is still a very pleasant place indeed' has some justification.

Although the borough is small, it has a central library and three branch libraries, so that no one is more than about ten minutes' walk from the nearest library building. Stoke Newington was one of the first boroughs to adopt the Public Libraries Act, which it did in 1890. The present central building was opened in 1892 and it now houses, among other facilities, a reading room, reference library (to accommodate 70 readers), lending library, children's library and two lecture halls. The total book stock in 1963 amounted to well over 128,000 volumes and there were nearly 1,600 gramophone records. Stoke Newington libraries are shut all day on Wednesdays (except the reference and reading rooms), open between 9 am and 8 pm on weekdays and until 5 pm on Saturdays. The Special Collection on Asian and African History is this borough's responsibility.

**Wandsworth** (population 347,442; 9,201 acres) is the largest of the 28 metropolitan boroughs and is a mainly residential area occupying the south-west quarter if the metropolis. It has some light industry and along the banks of the Thames and its tributary, the River Wandle, there are pockets of heavy industry, but most of its working population travel daily to central London and the City. Housing in its constituent districts (including, among others, Putney, Roehampton, Wandsworth proper, Tooting, Balham, parts of Clapham and Streatham) was put up in two main phases – by private developers who built extensively over the borough in the first ten years of the century, and by the local housing authorities on a large scale before and after the last war.

The borough has one central library and eleven branches, accommodating 554,000 books and (kept at the Balham and Putney branches) 6,800 gramophone records. The normal opening hours are 10 am to 8 pm, except on Saturdays (until 6 pm) and early closing days (1 pm on Wednesdays or Thursdays according to the part of the borough). As in Stepney, reference departments open at 9 am. The London Collection of works about General Archaeology, European History and Geography are housed in Wandsworth.

### The Londoners

Official figures provide many of the facts likely to bear on the public's relationships with the public library service – sheer numbers, for a start, but also the age structure of the population, its social class composition, the ages at which people left school or completed further education and, lastly, their countries of origin. It was important for the sample to include areas which were, on the face of it, propitious for effective relationships and others where that relationship was likely to be difficult.

The first 1961 Census figures were published after the sample for this enquiry was drawn, but they show (Table 1) which boroughs were having to cater for growing populations and which reflected the general decline in metropolitan London's population.

Table 1 Populations of seven London boroughs, 1951 and 1961*

| Borough | 1951 population | 1961 population | Increase/ decrease | Per cent change |
|---|---|---|---|---|
| Chelsea | 50,957 | 47,256 | − 3,701 | −8 |
| Finsbury | 33,370 | 32,887 | − 2,483 | −6 |
| Hampstead | 95,131 | 98,844 | + 3,713 | +4 |
| Lewisham | 227,576 | 221,753 | − 5,823 | −3 |
| Stepney | 98,858 | 92,000 | − 6,858 | −7 |
| Stoke Newington | 49,136 | 52,301 | + 3,165 | +6 |
| Wandsworth | 330,467 | 347,442 | +16,975 | +5 |

* The figures for this and subsequent tables are extracted or derived from Census 1951, London, General Register Office, HMSO, 1953, and from Census 1961, County of London Report, HMSO, 1962.

The different age structures of the seven populations (Table 2) have obvious implications for the extent of library use; it is worth noting, for instance, that eight per cent of Stoke Newington's and Finsbury's populations consisted of children under five, compared with Chelsea's five per cent. In terms of age, therefore, Chelsea had proportionately more potential library users. Furthermore, a library's 'performance' (and its responsibilities) may also be affected by the proportion of elderly people living in its area because the demand may change its nature and intensity. Here again, the variation is considerable, from 9·8 per cent in Stoke Newington to 14·6 per cent in Chelsea and 14·2 per cent in Finsbury.

Table 2 Age structure of the population of seven London boroughs, 1961

| Borough | Age in years (per cent) 0–4 | 5–14 | 15–24 | 25–44 | 45–64 | 65+ |
|---|---|---|---|---|---|---|
| Chelsea | 5·2 | 6·9 | 15·3 | 27·6 | 27·4 | 14·6 |
| Finsbury | 8·3 | 14·1 | 12·7 | 26·1 | 24·6 | 14·2 |
| Hampstead | 5·6 | 8·9 | 17·2 | 30·8 | 25·8 | 11·7 |
| Lewisham | 7·1 | 14·3 | 13·8 | 26·0 | 26·2 | 12·6 |
| Stepney | 7·6 | 14·2 | 14·3 | 28·7 | 24·6 | 10·3 |
| Stoke Newington | 8·1 | 13·2 | 15·1 | 28·9 | 24·9 | 9·8 |
| Wandsworth | 6·4 | 13·1 | 13·6 | 26·8 | 26·9 | 13·2 |

It is one of the purposes of education to familiarise people with books and accustom them to their use. It may be assumed that the more education people have had, the greater the importance of books in their lives. It does not follow, of course, that men and women who acknowledge that books are important to them will turn to public libraries to satisfy their need, but the marked inequalities in experience of education, between the residents in different boroughs, are likely to bear on the subject of this enquiry. Thus in Finsbury and Stepney, as Table 3 shows, 82 per cent of the population left school at 14 or younger – before or during adolescence, before their personalities and interests had crystallised – compared with 40 per cent in Hampstead.

Table 3 Terminal education ages of the occupied population of seven London boroughs, 1951*

| Borough | Percentages under 15 | 15 | 16 | 17–19 | over 20 | All stated ages† | Not stated |
|---|---|---|---|---|---|---|---|
| Chelsea | 47·1 | 10·7 | 12·1 | 19·4 | 10·7 | 26,191 | 971 |
| Finsbury | 82·5 | 8·9 | 4·7 | 2·9 | 1·0 | 20,060 | 497 |
| Hampstead | 40·2 | 12·1 | 15·7 | 19·7 | 12·3 | 49,902 | 3,299 |
| Lewisham | 65·6 | 14·2 | 11·9 | 6·0 | 2·3 | 105,592 | 3,741 |
| Stepney | 82·4 | 10·2 | 4·1 | 2·5 | 0·8 | 47,685 | 5,901 |
| Stoke Newington | 73·1 | 11·2 | 8·6 | 4·9 | 2·1 | 23,762 | 1,809 |
| Wandsworth | 63·0 | 2·6 | 12·6 | 8·5 | 3·3 | 149,190 | 14,433 |

* Except for age structure (Table 2), the detailed analysis of the 1961 figures was not available at the time of writing, so Tables 3–6 are derived from the 1951 Census.

† These figures equal 100 per cent for each borough.

Table 4 also shows the 'present' reinforcing the past – in Hampstead, when the 1951 Census figures were compiled, more than 12 per cent of the age group 20–24 was still undergoing full-time education, compared with only just over one in a hundred in Finsbury and Stepney. It is reasonable to expect such contrasts to have their consequences in the use or neglect of public libraries or in attitudes towards them.

These wide variations in educational background are associated, not surprisingly, with variations in occupation and social class. The Registrar-General's statistics distinguish five categories of men, occupied and

Table 4 Percentage of population of seven London boroughs in full-time education at different ages, 1951*

| Borough | Total pop. | 0–4 | 5–9 | 10–14 | 15 | 16 | 17–19 | 20–24 | 25+ |
|---|---|---|---|---|---|---|---|---|---|
| Chelsea | 10·7 | 2·2 | 89·4 | 96·6 | 51·6 | 38·3 | 19·0 | 9·8 | 1·00 |
| Finsbury | 12·3 | 6·8 | 94·9 | 98·4 | 28·3 | 10·3 | 2·4 | 1·1 | 0·15 |
| Hampstead | 10·9 | 2·2 | 92·3 | 98·1 | 57·9 | 42·9 | 25·2 | 12·5 | 1·00 |
| Lewisham | 13·9 | 1·7 | 93·1 | 97·3 | 52·2 | 28·4 | 8·3 | 3·1 | 1·60 |
| Stepney | 12·8 | 5·6 | 93·2 | 96·9 | 24·1 | 8·7 | 3·0 | 1·5 | 0·10 |
| Stoke Newington | 13·2 | 1·8 | 94·7 | 97·9 | 34·5 | 17·7 | 8·6 | 3·6 | 0·20 |
| Wandsworth | 12·2 | 1·4 | 91·0 | 95·8 | 48·4 | 27·3 | 10·4 | 4·3 | 0·30 |

* 1961 Census figures not yet available.

retired, over 15 years old – Class I, Professional; Class II, Intermediate; Class III, Skilled; Class IV, Partly Skilled; and Class V, Unskilled. Even people who know, say, the King's Road, Chelsea, and Mile End Road, Stepney, may be surprised at the social distance between them recorded in the 1951 data: out of every thousand males in Stepney, there were eight professional workers; in Chelsea there were 141. There were far more men in Classes I and II in Hampstead, per thousand of the adult population, than in any of the other six boroughs. No borough had such a high proportion of skilled workers as Stoke Newington.

Table 5 Class composition of the occupied male population of seven London boroughs, 1951*

| Borough | Numbers in Registrar-General's Categories† per thousand males over 15 I | II | III | IV | V |
|---|---|---|---|---|---|
| Chelsea | 141 | 188 | 439 | 110 | 122 |
| Finsbury | 12 | 78 | 520 | 163 | 227 |
| Hampstead | 119 | 262 | 465 | 80 | 74 |
| Lewisham | 35 | 159 | 588 | 97 | 121 |
| Stepney | 8 | 76 | 456 | 168 | 292 |
| Stoke Newington | 26 | 138 | 616 | 108 | 112 |
| Wandsworth | 48 | 173 | 568 | 98 | 113 |

* 1961 Census figures not yet available.

† The categories are defined as follows: I, Professional Occupations; II, Intermediate Occupations; III, Skilled Occupations; IV, Partly-skilled Occupations; V, Unskilled Occupations.

Finally, the people of London are increasingly, and to an extent understated by the 1951 figures, a polyglot population. It must matter to a public library system that a growing number of the people it might serve do not easily speak English, or have their own distinctive kinds of the language. Here again the populations of these seven boroughs showed marked differences (Table 6). In Hampstead 16·6 per cent of the residents were either of foreign nationality or naturalised; at the other end of the scale, only 1·5 per cent of the people in Lewisham came, at the time of the 1951 Census, from outside the Commonwealth, but it must be stressed that these figures understate the cosmopolitan complexion of the population in 1962 when the survey was carried out.

Table 6 Nationalities of population of seven London boroughs, 1951*

| Borough | Country of origin (percentage of total population) | | | | |
|---|---|---|---|---|---|
| | British† | Irish | Commonwealth and colonies | British (and naturalised) born abroad | Foreign and no nationality |
| Chelsea | 82·5 | 5·3 | 4·2 | 3·5 | 4·5 |
| Finsbury | 92·8 | 3·0 | 1·0 | 1·1 | 2·1 |
| Hampstead | 73·8 | 5·7 | 3·9 | 9·8 | 6·8 |
| Lewisham | 96·3 | 1·4 | 0·8 | 0·7 | 0·8 |
| Stepney | 87·2 | 2·0 | 2·2 | 2·6 | 6·0 |
| Stoke Newington | 89·0 | 2·1 | 1·0 | 3·8 | 4·1 |
| Wandsworth | 92·2 | 2·4 | 1·3 | 1·3 | 2·8 |

* 1961 Census figures not yet available.
† i.e. England, Wales, Scotland, Isle of Man, Channel Islands.

## Figures of membership

It ought in theory to be possible to set the chapters that follow in a context of figures reliably showing how many people in these seven boroughs were members of public libraries. There are two reasons why only approximations are available. First, it is a feature of the schemes of metropolitan library co-operation already alluded to, to permit a member of one borough's library to use his tickets in another; many people prefer to join the library nearest to where they work rather than the one near home.

This transfer amenity would, in itself, diminish the accuracy of some library statistics, enlarging the *clientèle* for libraries in office districts (especially Holborn), and reducing it in residential boroughs; but the second qualification to be remembered when approaching these statistics is more important: different chief librarians in the survey boroughs set a different value upon keeping accurate records. Some of them regard statistics as important indicators of their progress and some kind of objective account of their stewardship of public funds and resources, but at least one chief librarian asserted that those of his own figures which showed the number of registered readers and their ratio to the total population were quite useless. Where tickets remained valid for three or more years and there was a high turnover in population, membership figures became grossly inflated. In this librarian's view, the only figure to give a reliable guide to a library's 'performance' is the number of book issues per year.

Table 7 shows the total (reliable) number of books issued from each of the libraries in the seven boroughs in the year April 1962–March 1963; Table 8 shows the (much less reliable) number of registered readers per 1,000 of the population in each borough in March 1963.* Both tables include comparable figures for metropolitan London as a whole and for the great majority of county and non-county boroughs in the rest of the country (75 and 169 respectively) for which figures were available.

The differences between borough and borough in the survey may be

Table 7 Number of books issued from the libraries of seven London boroughs in the year April 1962–March 1963

| Borough | Population | Number of books issued | Issues per head of population |
|---|---|---|---|
| Chelsea | 48,550 | 554,600 | 11·4 |
| Finsbury | 33,020 | 338,466 | 10·2 |
| Hampstead | 98,240 | 1,342,590 | 13·7 |
| Lewisham | 222,170 | 2,304,498 | 10·4 |
| Stepney | 90,480 | 713,066 | 7·9 |
| Stoke Newington | 52,180 | 661,746 | 12·7 |
| Wandsworth | 347,906 | 3,709,737 | 10·7 |
| London total (28 boroughs) | 3,223,000 | 33,634,000 | 10·4 |
| Seventy-five county boroughs and 169 non-county boroughs (1961–62) | 20,768,000 | 188,856,000 | 9·1 |

* Tables 7–10 are based on figures supplied by the Association of Metropolitan Chief Librarians and from *Statistics of Public (Rate Supported) Libraries of Great Britain and Northern Ireland, 1961–62*, published by the Library Association, 1963.

Table 8 Number of registered library members per 1,000 of population of seven London boroughs at 31 March 1963

| Borough | Number of members | Members per 1,000 of population |
|---|---|---|
| Chelsea | 17,439 | 359 |
| Finsbury | 12,771 | 386 |
| Hampstead | 47,210 | 481 |
| Lewisham | 68,994 | 311 |
| Stepney | 16,005 | 177 |
| Stoke Newington | 14,860 | 285 |
| Wandsworth | 178,298 | 512 |
| London total (excluding Holborn) | 1,002,000 | 313 |
| Seventy-five county boroughs and 169 non-county boroughs (1962) | 5,967,000 | 287 |

smaller than they seem from these tables. The changes in registration/population ratios for the years 1961, 1962 and 1963 recorded in Table 9 show the shifts occurring through objective losses and gains and through idiosyncrasies of record keeping.* Although the relative positions of the boroughs changed over the three-year period, each borough consistently claimed about the same proportion of its residents as members.

Table 9 Number of registered library members per 1,000 of population of seven London boroughs, annually for 1961, 1962 and 1963

| Borough | Number of registered library members per 1,000 of population | | |
|---|---|---|---|
| | 1961 | 1962 | 1963 |
| Chelsea | 355 | 416 | 359 |
| Finsbury | 273 | 333 | 386 |
| Hampstead | 511 | 494 | 481 |
| Lewisham | 260 | 306 | 311 |
| Stepney | 182 | 174 | 177 |
| Stoke Newington | 269 | 268 | 285 |
| Wandsworth | 475 | 484 | 512 |
| All London boroughs (excluding Holborn) | 293 | 304 | 313 |

* A change in the loan period may also distort the figures; for instance, in April 1961, Stepney extended the period from two to four weeks, and recorded a drop of nine per cent in the number of issues during the subsequent year.

By the criterion of annual book issues per head, these librarians were evidently slightly more efficient during 1962–63 than the county and non-county boroughs taken as a whole. By the more familiar, but less reliable, criterion of members per thousand of the population, many of these library services were serving proportionately more of their public than the London average and, as a group, more than the national average (about one in three).

There is one further point about the library-public relationship that needs to be made at this stage: there is no direct connection between, on the one hand, the number of issues and the proportion of members, and on the other, the generosity with which the libraries were stocked and the amount that the boroughs were prepared to spend. A borough may spend much but spread it thinly over many members, or spend less but more generously in relation to the size of membership, or it may occupy some intermediate position. The areas sampled included instances of all three.*

Table 10 Lending stock and annual expenditure on books of seven London boroughs, April 1962–March 1963

| Borough | Lending stock Per head of population | Per member | Expenditure on books Per head of population | Per member |
|---|---|---|---|---|
| Chelsea | 1·80 | 5·0 | 3s 4d | 9s 4d |
| Finsbury | 2·75 | 7·1 | 8s 3d | 21s 2d |
| Hampstead | 2·01 | 4·2 | 3s 9d | 7s 10d |
| Lewisham | 1·57 | 5·0 | 3s 7d | 11s 7d |
| Stepney | 1·68 | 9·5 | 2s 8d | 14s 11d |
| Stoke Newington | 2·02 | 7·1 | 3s 11d | 13s 11d |
| Wandsworth | 1·49 | 2·9 | 3s 7d | 6s 11d |

The table (Table 10) lists such dissimilar boroughs as Finsbury, which spent substantially more than the other boroughs both per head of population and per member, had proportionately the largest lending stock, and was serving something like a quarter of its resident population; and Stepney, which although a relatively low spender, provided a most ample service to the fifth of the population which was in membership. Perhaps the implication of this table for policy is that there is much more to

* Library Committees may also attach special importance to the service they give to industrial and commercial users, and this might cause them, for example, to spend more on reference than on lending sections. This report does not deal at all with the libraries' relationships with such users.

improving the effectiveness with which libraries serve their constituents than glib recommendations simply to spend more would suggest. There has to be a strategy of spending, guided both by professional goals and by knowledge of the public's wishes and requirements.

This chapter has described the places (a mixture of dissimilar boroughs to sum up and represent the heterogeneous capital); their inhabitants (native and foreign born, solicitously and perfunctorily educated, occupationally administrative, productive and domestic); and their library services. These services varied in their success and lavishness, but collectively achieved rather more use by more users than the services run by boroughs in the rest of the country. The next chapter, which quotes the survey findings for the first time, will examine the public in finer detail by drawing two distinctions that the official figures do not make: first, not merely between members and non-members, but between those who are members, those who once were, and those who never have been; and secondly, between those who are members and those who use public libraries without being members.

Chapter 3

# Londoners interviewed

Figures from official sources about the number of people who belong to public libraries are a rough guide to the facts, rather than a faithful statistical mirror of them. The official figures for the seven selected boroughs (Table 8) show that from a fifth to a half of their resident populations were public library members (compared with a national average of nearly one in three).

## Members, former members and non-members

Although the proportion of *members* is known in broad terms, even within such limits the existing figures claim to speak only about current membership. It is also important to distinguish those who have once been members of a public library (*former members*) from those who have never been members (*non-members*). These distinctions are of interest in their own right, since they qualify such statements as 'most people must be, however transiently, registered members of a public library' (A. H. Bill, in the speech quoted on p. 5). But, furthermore, as it was necessary, for the purposes of this survey, to elicit different kinds of information from members, former members and non-members (in order, for instance, to study 'drop-out' and turnover), it was also necessary to be able to sort people into these three groups.

The survey was consequently organised in two stages – in the first contact was made systematically with a large sample of people in order to determine the incidence of membership, lapsed membership and abstention from membership in the adult population. In the second stage, some of the people interviewed for the first stage (501 of them) were asked to answer more questions according to the three groups to which they belonged. These people were also selected systematically so that the groups should be as equal as possible in size, and so that the entire second stage sample should be representative, by sex and occupation, of the seven borough populations. The procedure and the extent to which it succeeded are described in Appendix 2.

In the first stage, contact was made with 1,306 people in the seven boroughs. Interviewers were instructed to distinguish relationships with the library as follows:

> A *non-member* is a person who has *never* been a member of a *public* library.
> A *former member* is someone who used to belong to a public library but, for some reason, does so no longer.
> A *member* is one who holds a ticket for any public library, or one who considers himself still a member of a library even though technically he is not – i.e. his ticket may have expired. For example, on moving from one place to another, he may not have actually become a member of the local library, and even though his ticket to his former library may have expired, he may still consider himself a member. He should be taken as a member unless the period of lapse is more than twelve months.

Of the 1,306 people interviewed, 713 (54 per cent) were or had been public library members. Of these 713, there were 396 (30 per cent of the total sample) still in membership, while 317 (24 per cent of the total) had allowed their membership to lapse. The remaining 593 men and women (46 per cent) never had been members.

The survey conducted in 1959 by the Society of Young Publishers used a sample, stratified by age, sex and social status to be representative of the population of the Greater London area, and found that 54 per cent of all their informants had borrowed books from a public library at some time or other. RICA, using a quite different sampling technique in the last quarter of 1962, arrived at precisely the same figure. It is, therefore, stretching the word 'most' to say that most people must at some time or another have been public library members, and that turnover is caused by their dissatisfaction. Nearly half the adult population have never been enrolled anywhere as public library members. The proportion of current members in the population may be nearer one in three than the somewhat undisciplined figures in Table 8 imply. Those who had been members but were not members at the time of the survey amounted to nearly one in four. Whether this large minority was also a discontented one remains to be seen.

### Membership and use

Even if the official figures of participation are inflated, it may be objected that these findings understate the libraries' effective contact with their potential public. In the first place, it is fair to remember that the total population of a borough is not the same as the library's potential membership. Certain groups in the population have to be excluded. As Table 2 showed, children under four made up as many as eight per cent of the total population in two of the seven boroughs. There are also those people who are too old, or too ill, to read. Another group should perhaps be excluded because they do not know how to read. In 1956, not less than a quarter of the 15-year-old school population consisted of illiterate, semi-literate or backward readers.* Some of these pupils, when they left school, might appropriately be considered a special responsibility of the public library service, but the four per cent of that age group who were semi-literate (that is, had a pre-war reading age of less than nine years) cannot fairly be included in the service's potential public for book borrowing. This survey did not include any of the junior population, but the official ratios would be fairer if infants were deducted from the total population figures. The other groups mentioned – the too old, the too ill, or the too illiterate – were in fact reached to some extent in the survey, as will appear, though people living in institutions were not visited. But to leave out some of these groups altogether from the public library's potential membership is, indeed, to risk begging an important administrative question: should the remit of the public library system include hospitals, prisons and other places of retreat, as it already does in some places, or exclude them?

It may further be objected that the distinction drawn between members, former members and non-members is not wholly valid since anyone may make use of some of a library's facilities. Use and non-use are not necessarily co-extensive with membership and non-membership. B. Berelson noted, in *The Library's Public*,† that in America the libraries' *clientèle* is augmented by 20 per cent because of non-registered people who read books borrowed by members. He observed:

> There are several institutions in modern society which claim more than they do; in this respect the public library is doing more than it claims.

It was one purpose of the second stage of this survey to find out whether London's libraries are being similarly modest, and, if so, to what extent. There are, in short, two distinct ways in which people may or do use public libraries without being members. It is possible for both former members and non-members to read books borrowed by members; and it is also possible for them to use other facilities offered by the libraries – to read magazines or to consult reference books, for example. If the extent of this unrecorded use were substantial, librarians might feel a little less anxious about the two persons in three who do not appear in their records, and the one person in four who did once but does so no longer.

Out of the 501 respondents selected for interview in the second stage, 341 were non-members or former members. Of these 341, only 16 said they used reading room facilities, and 19 that they used the reference facilities for one reason or another. To put the same findings negatively,

* *Standards of Reading, 1948–56*, Ministry of Education. HMSO, 1957.

† New York, Columbia University Press, 1949, p. 110.

the great majority of people who do not belong to public libraries do not use them in these other ways at all. A supplementary question elicited the information that 26 of the 35 people concerned visited libraries intermittently, only nine of them going at fairly regular weekly or monthly intervals. These figures engender the suspicion that the library users outside the lending departments hardly constitute a separate, extra *clientèle*, and this is reinforced by the answers to a complementary question put to members. Of 160 members, 82 (about half) used their reference library and 39 (almost a quarter) used the reading room or its equivalent.

A further breakdown of the use of libraries by those not in membership shows that slightly more former members than those who never were members use the library, but the numbers are so small that this cannot be claimed with much certainty. What can be said is that, of the people who are not members of a library, only a small minority use its facilities – 12 per cent at the most generous estimate, and, more conservatively, something like three per cent (the regulars). In this respect the public library is not doing much more than it claims.

However, it is still possible that the figures on record under-estimate use because they cannot show how many people are reading books borrowed on other people's tickets – the particular practice to which Berelson drew attention, and facilitated by the right to borrow up to three or four books on one membership card. To get at this was slightly more complicated – non-members were asked whether they ever read books borrowed from a public library by other members of the household, and members were asked whether other people in the household read books which they borrowed. Where members answered 'yes', it was then necessary, of course, to ask whether these 'other people' were members too.

Out of 341 people not in membership, there were 54 (15·8 per cent) who said that they read books borrowed by other people, and former members were slightly more likely to do this than those who had never joined a public library. Out of 158 members, 70 said that others in the same household read books which they had borrowed, and in 23 of the households concerned (14·8 per cent) these others were not members. The two sets of replies cannot be combined because former members and non-members answered for themselves as individuals, whereas members were speaking about their households. It seems reasonable to estimate, however, that something like 15 per cent of the public in these boroughs are reading library books, without appearing in the statistics of library registration. In this respect, at least, librarians may resist the charge that their figures are 'grossly inflated', and share with their American colleagues the credit for claiming less than they do.

There is one final aspect of membership and use which is relevant here, since it is the contrary possibility to those considered so far – namely, that far from members being outnumbered by users, users might turn out to be at any one time a minority group within the membership – a fifth was A. H. Bill's estimate (see p. 5). This is a difficult possibility to check, for how are 'use' and 'one time' to be defined? The library members were asked a question which hindsight shows could have been better worded, but the answers throw some light on this, in so far as 'regularity' would be one of the main tests of effective use. The question was 'About how often do you go to the library?'; Table 11 summarises the answers, analysed in the categories used on the spot by the interviewers. Respondents to such

Table 11 Frequency of members' library visits

| Interval | Number | Per cent |
|---|---|---|
| At least weekly | 45 | 28 |
| About once a fortnight | 51 | 32 |
| Say once a month | 37 | 23 |
| Once in three months | 8 | 5 |
| Less often | 1 | 1 |
| Intermittently | 18 | 11 |

a question are quite likely to be mistaken about the frequency of their visits, and the suggested intervals were worded rather loosely, so that too much precision should not be read into the figures. Nevertheless, it is reasonable to expect most people who said they went every week – for instance, as part of the regular major shopping expedition, which several of them mentioned – to be reasonably accurate, and these were well over a quarter of all members.

Those who went to the library at least twice a month were a substantial majority (60 per cent), and those whose contact was really tenuous were rare. The 'intermittent' users included people who made intensive use of the library from time to time as their special interests required. It looks as though A. H. Bill's depreciation of the libraries' performance was unduly pessimistic.

To summarise this chapter: just over 1,300 men and women were contacted. A little over half of them had at some time in their lives belonged to a public library, and nearly a third of them still did. Conversely, a little under half of them had never been members of public libraries. Interviews with a smaller group showed that hardly any non-members or former members made use of the library facilities which are open to all, but nearly one in seven of them continued to benefit directly from the libraries' existence, by reading books borrowed on other people's tickets.

Dissatisfaction with the service may cause members to let their membership expire; it can hardly explain why nearly half the adult population have never joined. Examination of the reasons for this abstention must start with the logical possibility, however unlikely it may seem, that some people just do not know about public libraries, and with the likelihood that they do not know much about what public libraries have to offer. These matters are dealt with in the next chapter.

Chapter 4

# Public awareness of libraries

It will be apparent that this report is not a critical or comparative study of the specific facilities available to public library users in London; but some brief indication of available facilities is called for, since they may affect the relationships which the public have with the library service, and their attitudes towards it.

## Facilities

The size of the bookstocks and gramophone collections in the seven boroughs have already been given in Chapter 2. When the survey was conducted it was, of course, possible to borrow up to three books at a time in Chelsea and Lewisham; up to four in Finsbury, Stoke Newington and Wandsworth; and up to six in Hampstead and Stepney. In four of the boroughs students or people going on holiday could borrow books for longer than the normal two- to four-week period. It was possible for members in all of them to renew books by telephone, and Chelsea was installing an automatic telephone so that this could be done at any time of night or day. At Finsbury Central there was a 'night safe' for books to be returned after closing time.

In principle all the books owned by all the libraries were available to a member of any one of them, and those of all the other London boroughs, through the metropolitan libraries' inter-lending scheme. A network of such schemes enables readers to borrow almost any book, British or foreign – some ephemera excepted – through their own local branches.

As noted, all seven systems (but not all branches) lent gramophone records. They also lent sheet music, scores and maps; all except Wandsworth lent holiday guides; members in Lewisham could, if they wished, borrow paintings and reproductions. Each of these library authorities ran exhibitions or provided accommodation for them; all did the same for film shows (except Hampstead) and lectures (except Chelsea). There were record recitals in the libraries of Finsbury, Stepney, Stoke Newington and Wandsworth.

Apart from their stock for reference or use on the premises, library members could borrow periodicals from Lewisham and Stepney; pamphlets from Chelsea, Finsbury, Lewisham and Stepney; film strips from Finsbury, Lewisham, Stepney and Wandsworth; and slides from all but Hampstead and Stoke Newington. All the librarians issued reading lists (short lists on particular subjects or monthly lists of new acquisitions), or were willing to prepare bibliographies on request. They had installed a photocopying service everywhere except Stoke Newington. The residents of Wandsworth could read back numbers of *The Tooting and Balham Gazette* on microfilm.

At that time, none of the boroughs lent tapes, talking books or pottery (the mention of which prompted one librarian to ask 'Where is it going to end?'), but it will already be clear from these facts about facilities (which are not at all exhaustive) that there are many different ways in which the resources of the libraries in these seven boroughs can be exploited by interested members of the public, when they know what is available to them.

## Awareness of location and facilities

The relationship between *awareness* of a service and *use* of it is not simple. If people do not know where the public library is, or if they do not know what facilities it offers, then their ignorance may not merely discourage them from becoming library users; it may inhibit the possibility from ever entering their heads. It may be said, on the other hand, that if people were interested then they would find out, but this is to over-simplify. The initiatives of resourceful men depend to a great extent on the fact that other people have taken the trouble, from school onwards, to supply them with information about possible choices to be made. The general impression created by the replies in this survey is that while nearly everyone knows something about the public library service, they do not know nearly enough about it or about the sheer range of its amenities for present demand to be regarded as anything like the limit.

Since awareness of public library facilities was related to the localities in which the interviews were conducted, it was necessary first to find out how many respondents were too new to the district for it to be fair to expect them to know the answers to some questions. In fact, 91·5 per cent of the respondents had lived in the survey areas for at least 12 months. The proportion of newcomers was more than twice as great among those not in membership as among members.

There can surely be no simpler test of awareness than the question 'Can you tell me where the nearest library is?' ('Nearest' was interpreted either as nearest in distance, or as most accessible or most convenient to the respondent.) The interviewers knew the possible answers and hence were able to distinguish three types of reply – 'definitely knows', 'knows vaguely' or 'does not know'. Only 43 people in the entire second-stage sample of 501 (nine per cent) did not know where their nearest library was, whereas 395 (79 per cent) knew definitely. Naturally, the proportions of those knowing vaguely or not at all were larger among those who were not in membership (see Table 12).

Table 12 The sample: knowledge of location of nearest library

| | Members | | Former members | | Non-members | | Totals | |
|---|---|---|---|---|---|---|---|---|
| | No. | Per cent | No. | Per cent | No. | Per cent | No. | Per cent |
| Definitely knows | 154 | 96 | 110 | 77 | 134 | 68 | 398 | 79 |
| Knows vaguely | 5 | 3 | 22 | 15 | 33 | 17 | 60 | 12 |
| Does not know | 1 | 1 | 12 | 8 | 30 | 15 | 43 | 9 |
| Totals | 160 = 100 | | 144 = 100 | | 197 = 100 | | 501 = 100 | |

Among those who were vague about the location of the library there were five members, and one member did not know where it was, the explanation being that a small number of members were housebound and someone else went to the library on their behalf. A small number (eight people or five per cent of all members) were not enrolled in the library nearest to where they lived. (A further 14 per cent were enrolled both in their local library and in another borough's, usually the borough in which they worked.)

Most people, then, did know where their nearest library was and were usually quite definite about it. Whether someone *uses* the library or not is, however, likely to be affected by his knowledge of the services it offers. Consequently, a selection was made from the range of facilities and everyone was asked whether the local library provided: a separate room for children's books; a reading room with newspapers and magazines; a room for studying or for children's homework; a gramophone record lending department; a lecture room (whether lectures were held in the library); and an information service (whether the library would look up all kinds of information for anyone interested).

Respondents answered 'yes', 'no' or 'don't know'. In theory, it would be possible to check all the 'yes' and 'no' answers against the facts. In practice, this proved far too complicated, and it was assumed that those who answered 'yes' and 'no' knew definitely (although many of them may, in fact, have been wrong); hence the 'don't knows' were the most reliable answers and these provide a *minimum* measure of the public's lack of awareness of library facilities (Table 13).

Table 13 The sample: lack of awareness of library facilities

| | Members | Former members | Non-members | Total not in membership | Total |
|---|---|---|---|---|---|
| Number in sample | 160 | 144 | 197 | 341 | 501 |
| Facility | Percentages | | | | |
| Information | 16 | 38 | 55 | 47 | 37 |
| Reading room | 9 | 35 | 55 | 47 | 35 |
| Children's department | 8 | 26 | 41 | 35 | 26 |
| Gramophone records | 34 | 62 | 79 | 72 | 60 |
| Study space | 35 | 70 | 75 | 72 | 60 |
| Lectures | 46 | 65 | 75 | 71 | 63 |

How this measure of unawareness is judged must partly depend on the particular facility. For example, information services have been in existence very much longer than, say, collections of gramophone records, and most librarians consider the provision of information more central to their main function. Or again, although gramophone records are in principle available throughout a borough, the records themselves are normally housed in and loaned only from central libraries, and people who habitually use branch libraries may not know this.

However, some startling gaps in public knowledge were revealed. For some librarians, providing information is second in importance only to lending books: yet it seems as if more than a third of the public is unaware that the libraries' resources are at their disposal. At least 16 per cent of the members did not know.* This helps to explain something that disturbed A. H. Bill in the speech quoted in Chapter 1. He was prompted by an examination of letters to women's magazines and technical periodicals to wonder:

> Why, for example, did someone requiring the addresses of makers of ultrasonic cleaning equipment have to write to a commercial journal for them? Did

* Those few who were enrolled in libraries elsewhere might have been better informed had the question not specified 'local' library.

> enquirers wanting publications on powder metallurgy, a Spanish-English shipbuilding dictionary, old copies of the periodical *American Machinist* (some random examples) overlook their public library service – or find it wanting? . . . Even with the inadequacies of our present service, we are able to find the answers to most questions of this kind, and we could and would gladly give them to everyone. But we are not asked.

The annual reports produced by the seven borough librarians show that they can cope with questions quite as esoteric as these examples. It seems likely that libraries are overlooked, rather than found inadequate. Many people prefer to write to an anonymous adviser, but when even 16 per cent of the members do not think of a library as a place to find out, or to be told, almost anything (from train times to details of the average input for ribbon microphones), it is hardly surprising that nearly half those not in membership do not either. In summary, nearly two members of the public in every five do not know about this traditional and well-established service.

It is perhaps not so surprising that there is little use of reading rooms except by members when nearly half of those not in membership do not know whether reading rooms exist; six people in every ten were apparently unaware that these libraries lend gramophone records (as they all do) – even a third of the members did not know this, and nor did half the youngest people (15–20 years). As already suggested, this may be due partly to the fact that many people are unaware of the difference, in terms of immediately accessible facilities, between branch and central libraries. Answers to another question show that 22 per cent of library members did not know whether their nearest library was the central library or a branch: if it were a branch they might not realise what they were missing.

Maximum exploitation of the library service in London depends not only on a branch user realising that the resources of the central library and those of other boroughs are at his disposal, but also on the public knowing that if they belong to a library in one borough, they may borrow books from other libraries throughout the metropolis. Not everyone travels about the region, of course, but everyone was asked 'Do you know whether you can use libraries in other boroughs?' 'Yes' was taken to be the right answer, which it is in principle, even though in practice different charging systems reduce the ease with which other libraries can be used. Thirty-seven per cent of the members gave the wrong answer or did not know (but, unexpectedly, 35 per cent of those who were never members gave the right answer).

Although many librarians may feel that their rich and varied resources are well used, the evidence from this survey shows that there are simple facts about amenities of which the public – even many who go in and out

Table 14 The sample: knowledge of inter-availability of library tickets

| | Members | Former | Non-members | Total not in membership | Total |
|---|---|---|---|---|---|
| Number in sample | 160 | 144 | 196 | 340 | 500 |
| Answers | Percentages | | | | |
| Can use | 63 | 51 | 35 | 42 | 48·5 |
| Cannot use | 8 | 15 | 12 | 13 | 12 |
| Don't know | 29 | 34 | 53 | 45 | 39·5 |
| Total wrong answers | 37 | 49 | 65 | 58 | 51·5 |

for books – are quite unaware. The scale on which there is a widespread lack of knowledge is made evident by this sample.

**Lines for future enquiries**

Old hunches about what the public does not know can now assume a degree more accuracy, but there are still many questions of interest to librarians and educationists which it would be useful to have answered – whether, for instance, the people in each borough known to be so different in important respects are equally ill-informed; whether well-educated men and women are as much in the dark as the less-educated; whether older people (benefiting, perhaps, from experience) are more aware than younger people (who might, on the other hand, gain from deliberate introduction to library use in schools). Further research would be needed to provide more reliable evidence on these particular issues than can be inferred from the relatively small sample drawn for this survey.*

It so happens that the people in this sample who did not know where their nearest library was came, in fact, from all seven boroughs and all walks of life. The proportions of people who did not know about library information services were similar in all occupational groups, whether they were directors and executives or manual labourers. Young people knew about the information facility less often than their elders, and they were hardly more aware of gramophone record collections. They were much less likely than people over 35 to know that libraries are places where magazines can be read. But these are only hints of what might be in-

* Comments based on the sample survey in this and later chapters are definite or cautious according to whether differences in the data were found to be statistically significant or not.

vestigated by subsequent research, drawing on a larger sample for the purpose.

Similar possibilities emerge from this sample's knowledge of the inter-availability of library membership tickets – a more sophisticated matter but an instance of the kind of knowledge which will be increasingly needed in the future to take maximum advantage of library services in this country. In this sample, the men knew about inter-availability of tickets more often than women, executives more often than workers, the longest educated than those who left school early, the young than the over-35s. These facts may, however, simply be facts about these 500 people, not generalisations about Londoners. They are suggestive, not probative. What they help to reveal most of all, perhaps, is the extent to which lack of public knowledge about libraries and their facilities is matched by an ignorance by the public library service of the public it is meant to be serving.

**Conclusion**

There is, then, a very tiny fraction of the population which does not even know where the nearest public library is. There are larger, sometimes impressively large, minorities who do not know the basic facilities which public libraries make available, and these minorities include people who are registered members. The differences in awareness between members, former members and those who never were members are, understandably, very marked; they may, therefore, be a guide to library authorities who wish to decide whether, for example, to try to increase the use made of libraries by present members, or whether to try extending their services to a larger number of people.

In either case, the effectiveness of the service and the directions in which it needs to develop, as well as the way in which it is promoted, depend in part on knowing more about the public, in particular knowing what it is that distinguishes someone who chooses to join a public library from someone who does not.

Chapter 5

# The nature of the public

So far, this report has tried to determine the actual extent of library membership and use, and it has examined public awareness of libraries and the facilities they offer. Both these endeavours presuppose that librarians wish to enlarge their effective contact with the public, and that more people might wish to use public libraries or to make more versatile use of them than they do. But it has not been assumed that librarians should not consider themselves really successful until practically everyone is in continuous membership, nor that everybody wants to use public libraries, and still less that everyone ought to be a public library user. The question underlying the whole of this report is not 'How can non-members be converted into members?' but 'Are the libraries serving as many people as they could, as well as they might?'

## The limits to effective contact

It could be argued that, although there are no doubt ways in which most public library services might be improved, the limits to effective contact with the public in any particular catchment area are set by that public. Evidence for this argument is provided by Tables 3 and 4 (Census data about the education of the seven boroughs' inhabitants) in juxtaposition with Table 8 (ratios of registered library members to total population). The Census data shows for instance that the people of Hampstead are very much better educated than the people of Stepney, and while graduate residents abound in the one borough they are hard to come by in the other. The difference is so great that it is hardly necessary to look further for an explanation of the different registration-population ratios in the two places. Whereas in Hampstead it might be enough to have a collection of books, open your doors and then step back to control the hordes of eager readers, in Stepney probably every enrolled reader has to be worked for, and hard.

No doubt this caricature contains a truth, but it obscures the possibilities for growth. The previous chapter gave evidence that many people have a limited idea of what a public library can offer them, and these people include those who have already taken the step of joining. For the libraries to 'enlarge their effective contact' could mean intensive development – increasing the use of a range of facilities by making the members more aware of them. But it could also mean extensive development – increasing the number of people choosing to use libraries and become members. The Census data do no more than imply a warning that the ease with which this is accomplished may vary from place to place, as may the extent of penetration; the sample data, on the other hand, offer grounds for believing some extensive development to be possible. The men and women who are currently members of public libraries are by no means the only people who might like to be.

### Education and membership

Analysis of the data from the survey confirms that the length of education people have had is a very powerful predictor of whether they will also be public library members (Table 15). There is evidently much truth in the aphorism of André Maurois (quoted by Christopher Chataway in the House of Commons) that education is 'but a key to open the doors of libraries'.*

Table 15 The sample: age of completing full-time education

| | Members | Former | Non-members | Total* |
|---|---|---|---|---|
| Number in sample | 160 | 144 | 195 | 499 |
| Age finished | Percentages | | | |
| Under 14 | 2 | 3 | 10 | 5 |
| 14 | 38 | 46 | 57 | 48 |
| 15 or 16 | 25 | 31 | 17 | 24 |
| 17 or 18 | 14 | 10 | 7 | 10 |
| 19 or 20 | 5 | 3 | 1 | 3 |
| 21 or over | 12 | 6 | 5 | 8 |
| Not yet finished | 4 | 1 | 1 | 2 |

* Two people had no formal education.

The striking regularity with which library membership can be correlated with length of education is made more explicit by grouping people into those who left school before they were 15, those who left at 15 or 16, and those who stayed on in full-time education after 17 (Table 16).

* Mr Chataway was moving the Second Reading of the Public Libraries and Museums Bill, 5 February 1964.

Table 16 The sample: age of completing full-time education in summary

| | Members | Former | Non-members | Total* |
|---|---|---|---|---|
| Number in sample | 160 | 144 | 195 | 499 |
| Age finished | Percentages | | | |
| Under 15 | 40 | 49 | 67 | 53 |
| 15 or 16 | 25 | 31 | 17 | 24 |
| 17 or over | 35 | 20 | 14 | 23 |

* Two people had no formal education.

The influence of education is manifest, and yet the influence of education is not absolute. Common sense expectations are confirmed: for instance, a far higher proportion of members than of those not in membership experienced prolonged education, and nearly seven in every ten of those men and women who have never been members left school before their fifteenth birthday. The majorities are found in Table 16 where they would be expected; but it is the minorities, the exceptional people, that are interesting and challenging, the well-educated person who never sets foot in his library, the poorly-educated one who is a regular reader. Table 16 can be studied both for its demonstration of the rule and for its revelation of the many exceptions to it.

Forty per cent of the members also left school before they were 15, and 20 per cent of the people who have given up being members were educated to 17 years of age and more. Seven per cent of those who never were members were educated until they were at least 19.

When the sample is analysed according to the type of full-time education, the same trend is confirmed, but the same anomalies appear.

Table 17 The sample: type of establishment at which full-time education was completed or is continuing

| | Members | Former | Non-members | Total* |
|---|---|---|---|---|
| Number in sample | 137 | 135 | 162 | 434 |
| Type of establishment | Percentages | | | |
| Higher, further | 19·7 | 9·0 | 8·6 | 12·2 |
| Grammar, public schools | 19·0 | 24·4 | 8·0 | 16·6 |
| Secondary modern, elementary | 61·3 | 66·6 | 83·4 | 71·2 |

* The figures exclude two people who had no formal education, forty-two who were educated abroad, and twenty-three others educated in circumstances which were too ambiguously described to classify (e.g. 'Private college').

As might be expected, not only the length but also the type of education is important in the making of the sort of person who joins a public library. But, though important, the kind of school attended is not invincible. Ex-secondary modern and ex-elementary school children account for well over half the members of these public libraries, and there are a number of graduates and others comparably educated who, for one reason or another, are not, or never have been, members. (It might be expected that the highly educated non-member would probably be registered with, say, the London Library or with some specialist library. In fact, membership of any kind of non-public library – popular/commercial as well as specialist – is so rare that it can be discounted. Out of 501 people, only eight belonged to specialist libraries – including two non-members of public libraries – and 11 to subscription libraries – of whom ten were non-members.)

Clearly, then, the length and type of education are important, but equally clearly they are crude indices; there are good and bad schools of all kinds, school years can be wasted or well-spent, endured or enjoyed. Although these are subtleties, an attempt was made to discover whether they had force on any scale by asking people how they felt about their schools, and also whether their school had tried to encourage them to use public libraries.

First, people were asked: 'How do you look back on your schooldays, on the whole?' They were shown a card with five statements on it, asked which of them came closest to their own feelings, and told that the statements were about whether they liked being at school, not about whether they thought they learned much. These were the five statements:

1. I liked them very much
2. I liked them quite a bit
3. They were all right, but nothing special
4. I didn't like them much
5. I disliked them very much.

Next, they were asked to choose one of five statements which were about whether they thought they had learned much:

1. I learned a great deal that was useful to me
2. I learned quite a bit
3. School was all right, but nothing special
4. They didn't teach me all that much
5. They taught me hardly anything.

(The emphasis was changed in the last two statements to protect the self-esteem of the people being questioned.)

There seems to be little difference between the answers of members and non-members on the first scale – whether, on the whole, they liked being at school or not. Indeed, those not in membership were slightly more likely to have enjoyed their schooldays than members, but the difference is not significant. However, on the second scale – whether they felt they had learned much – the three groups were strikingly different. Members and former members had a much more positive attitude towards their education than non-members. In Tables 18(A) and (B), the first two statements on each scale are combined as 'Positive', and the last three as 'Negative'.

Table 18(a) The sample: attitudes to schools

| | Members | Former | Non-members | Total* |
|---|---|---|---|---|
| Number in sample | 160 | 144 | 195 | 499 |
| Attitudes | Percentages | | | |
| Positive | 57·5 | 64·6 | 61·5 | 61·1 |
| Negative | 42·5 | 35·4 | 38·5 | 38·9 |

* Two people had no formal education.

Table 18(b) The sample: attitudes to learning

| | Members | Former | Non-members | Total* |
|---|---|---|---|---|
| Number in sample | 160 | 143 | 195 | 498 |
| Attitudes | Percentages | | | |
| Positive | 76·9 | 77 | 52·5 | 71·3 |
| Negative | 23·1 | 23 | 37·5 | 28·7 |

* Two people had no formal education, and one answer could not be classified.

It may be that some people never join libraries because they regard the library as an extension of school, or as making similar demands on them as school, and they believe these demands to be beyond their competence. Responses to the second scale were often in fact expressions of people's attitudes to themselves rather than to their schools. Many people who it would seem had acquired very little knowledge at school, comparatively speaking, said that they had learned a great deal there that was *useful to them.* It seems reasonable to infer that non-members are likely to be people who doubt (whether for justifiable or mistaken reasons is not here the point) their capacity to learn, even though it is known that many of those who do join libraries borrow books for their entertainment and not at all out of studiousness.

While positive attitudes towards learning at school are closely associated with library membership, current or past, it should be noted once more that the exceptions make up a large minority – nearly a quarter of the members and former members joined public libraries despite the feeling that they had learned little at school, and over half the non-members felt they had learned 'quite a bit' or more.

School should be the place where people learn how to learn, and where they are acquainted with the resources that are available for their pleasure as well as for their continuing education. Learning how to learn means both knowing about resources, and cultivating habits of initiative. Obviously, much more is involved than just having the initiative to use a public library and knowing what it offers, but to a large extent whether or not the schools succeed in strengthening personal autonomy may be judged by this criterion. An attempt was made, therefore, to discover the extent to which the schools had made deliberate attempts to encourage these respondents to use public libraries and whether their efforts had been successful.

The particular form of words used ('Did your school try to encourage you to become a public library user?') meant relying not only on people's memories, but also on their candour. It was the question that came nearest to implying a bias in favour of using a public library. However, by this stage in the interview, a permissive atmosphere and a relationship of confidence had usually been created, and there is no reason to doubt the sincerity of the replies, or, in particular, to suspect that non-members were tempted to minimise any efforts their schools might have made.

The replies illuminate two interconnected issues. They help to describe the kinds of people who become members of public libraries, but they also afford some assessment of whether schools have been doing one of their main tasks effectively, and whether their performance is improving over the years.

The question about school encouragement was put to 498 men and women in the sample.* Of these, just under half referred to some form of encouragement – the general atmosphere in the school, the influence of particular teachers, the example of a school library, or specially organised class visits to public libraries. Teachers were, understandably, mentioned most often. It would be reasonable to expect or hope that these influences would be relatively stronger among younger people, and among those staying on at school. The younger generations in the sample do in fact show a 13 per cent 'lead' over their elders, which suggests that schools may be improving (although, of course, the difference could be due to fresher memories), and those whose education went on after the age of 15

* Two people had attended no schools and one elderly respondent was too tired to answer by this stage.

acknowledge school encouragement to use libraries 16 per cent more often than those who left school before 15 (Table 19).

Table 19 The sample: extent of encouragement by school to use libraries, in different age groups

| | Age-group 15–35 | 36+ | School-leaving age Under 15 | 15+ | Total Sample* |
|---|---|---|---|---|---|
| Number in sample | 182 | 312 | 346 | 144 | 498 |
| Form of encouragement | Percentages | | | | |
| Any form of encouragement | 49 | 36 | 36 | 52 | 43 |
| Teachers | 30 | 26 | 24 | 33 | 28 |
| School libraries | 40 | 15 | 16 | 42 | 25 |
| Class visits | 9·5 | 5 | 6·5 | 7 | 6·5 |

* For discrepancies in sample and sub-sample totals, see notes to previous tables.

Staying on at school and access to a school library make a perceptible difference to the extent to which schools put people on the way to becoming culturally resourceful.

The reluctant ratepayer and the harassed teacher, who must sometimes wonder whether what happens in school ever has any long-term effect, will be joined, however, by the pragmatic public librarian, in wanting to know whether school encouragement leads to action. The short answer is 'yes': if the efforts of schools made little or no difference, then the en-

Table 20 The sample: extent of encouragement by school to use libraries, by library relationship

| | Members | Former | Past and present members | Non-members | Total* |
|---|---|---|---|---|---|
| Number in sample | 160 | 144 | 304 | 194 | 498 |
| Form of encouragement | Percentages | | | | |
| Any form of encouragement | — | 54 | 48 | — | — |
| Teachers | 26 | 42 | 34 | 18 | 28 |
| School libraries | 29·5 | 32 | 31 | 15 | 25 |
| Class visits | 4·5 | 10 | 7 | 6 | 6·5 |

* For discrepancies in sample and sub-sample totals, see note to previous tables.

couraged and not-encouraged would be found more or less evenly spread among the members, the former members and the non-members. This is emphatically not so.

Only 23 people in the entire sample said that they had been taken to look at public libraries, and, although this is a small number from which to generalise, it is not surprising to find that such occasional, perhaps once-only, visits seem to make little difference to whether someone actually joins a library or not, compared with the relatively strong, continuous influence of teachers and of school libraries. Past and present members quoted them twice as often as those who never joined.

People are, therefore, more likely to join a public library, at some time in their lives, if they stay on longer at school or in full-time education; if they go to a grammar-type or public school; if they feel that they learned something valuable at school; and if they are encouraged by their teachers to be interested in books, or by the presence of a school library to recognise a library as a familiar and useful institution. But this is to speak of statistical regularities, not of predestination: there are large minorities whose decisions – to join, to lapse, to stay away altogether – are not determined by these regularities.

## Other influences on membership

So far this chapter has concentrated on the effects of education on library membership, because of its obvious relevance, but a description of the kinds of people who belong or do not belong to public libraries must obviously take account of other characteristics. It is of professional and public interest to know whether the libraries are catering for a cross-section of the public, or whether their membership is heavily weighted with, say, women, or the elderly, or the poor or, even perhaps (remembering A. P. Herbert's polemics), the prosperous.* Librarians can observe the kinds of people who use a particular library, but observation is unlikely to provide an accurate analysis of whether the composition of library membership reflects the composition of the resident or working population.

In Tottenham, Mass Observation found in 1947 that 'men and women belong to an equal extent; if anything, women more frequently hold tickets than men'.† On the other hand, a survey in Derby some years

* Thelwell's cartoon illustration in Sir Alan Herbert's Hobart Paper shows the servants of the Rolls-Royce set staggering out of the public squalor of their 'Free Library' laden with tomes. *Libraries: Free-for-All?* A. P. Herbert, Institute of Economic Affairs, 1962.

† *Reading in Tottenham*, *op. cit.*

later* showed that 27 per cent of the men interviewed borrowed books from a public library compared with 24 per cent of the women. In the seven boroughs where this survey was conducted, 37 per cent of the men were members, whereas only 28 per cent of the women belonged to libraries. Conversely, the proportion of women who had never been members was slightly greater than the proportion of men. Yet this difference is not, in itself, statistically significant, and it seems reasonable to conclude that libraries have an equal appeal to men and women (Table 21).†

Table 21 The sample: library relationship by sex

| | Members Percentages | Former | Non-members | Total | Number in sample |
|---|---|---|---|---|---|
| Men | 36·8 | 28·1 | 35·1 | 100 | 231 |
| Women | 27·8 | 29·3 | 42·9 | 100 | 270 |

The frequency and intensity with which many librarians discuss devices to lure 'reluctant teenagers' into their sphere of influence indicates a belief that young people are conspicuously absent from the ranks of members. Library members do not, it is true, constitute more than a minority of the 15–20 age-group, but then they are no more than a minority in any age-group. Young people do, in fact, seem slightly more likely to be members than people at any other age. This is not to conclude that special efforts to attract young people are misconceived, but that such efforts ought not to be inspired by a misreading of the situation.

There is ample evidence that people of pensionable age tend to withdraw from social life, and although going to the library is a more individual activity than belonging to a club or attending a class, it exemplifies the same trend.‡ This may be, in part, an indirect reflection of the educational factor since both the immobility and the incapacity of people over 65 are popularly exaggerated. That limited education rather than age, as such, is more likely to be the determining factor in use of a library is suggested by

* *The Communication of Ideas*, T. Cauter and J. S. Downham, Chatto & Windus for Reader's Digest, 1954.

† See Appendix 2. The method and the sample.

‡ See, *inter alia*, *Education and Retirement*, Brian Groombridge, National Institute of Adult Education, 1960; *Social Policies for Old Age*, Barbara Shenfield, Routledge & Kegan Paul, 1957.

the large proportion of people in the senior age ranges who have never been members, compared with those who have allowed their membership to lapse. Membership seems, in fact, most likely to lapse during the family-rearing years. These findings (Table 22) confirm, in detail, the broad conclusions of the Derby survey, which also recorded that numbers of library book-borrowers decreased with increasing age.*

Table 22 The sample: library relationship by age

| | Members | Former | Non-members | Total* |
|---|---|---|---|---|
| Number in sample | 157 | 141 | 196 | 494 |
| Age groups | Percentages | | | |
| 15–20 | 10 | 6·5 | 6 | 8 |
| 21–35 | 26·5 | 34·5 | 28 | 30 |
| 36–55 | 44·5 | 34 | 32 | 36 |
| 56–65 | 10 | 14 | 17·5 | 14 |
| 66+ | 9 | 11 | 16·5 | 12 |

* Seven people gave no information about age.

The occupational distribution of the sample presents a picture more complex than that sometimes offered by self-critical members of the profession (such as D. E. Gerard, quoted on page 5, who feared that the library's public came from a narrow band in the middle of the middle class). It is obvious from Table 23 that professional men and women, and others with considerable executive responsibility, appear more frequently among the ranks of library members than in the public as a whole. It is also apparent that more than half of those who have never been members belong to the three least skilled occupational groups. It is true, therefore, that the public libraries' *clientèle* shows a marked middle-class bias. But this truth should not obscure the fact that the members are drawn almost evenly from all the occupational groups. There may be some reassurance in the discovery that there are almost as many 'workers' as 'professionals' and 'executives' in membership; the disquiet comes from recollecting their relative numbers in the population. Both poles of the antithesis need to be kept in view, however: it cannot help the libraries' work to accuse them of catering 'only for a self-conscious minority' of middle class people, with the possible implication that a working class public cannot be reached;

* Library book-borrowers in age-groups: 16–24 (35 per cent), 25–54 (25 per cent), 55–69 (18 per cent). Table 62, *The Communication of Ideas, op. cit.*

and yet it needs to be stressed that the 'success' of a library, and its methods of relating to the people in its area, will in fact depend to a large degree on the social composition of the neighbourhood.

Table 23 The sample: library relationship by occupation

| | Members | Former | Non-members | Total* |
|---|---|---|---|---|
| Number in sample | 142 | 136 | 184 | 462 |
| Occupational group | Percentages | | | |
| 1 and 2 | 22·6 | 13·2 | 8·1 | 14·1 |
| 3 | 23·2 | 22·8 | 17·4 | 20·8 |
| 4 | 21·1 | 17·6 | 16·8 | 18·2 |
| 5 | 16·1 | 19·8 | 22·8 | 20·1 |
| 6 and 7 | 17·0 | 26·4 | 34·3 | 26·6 |

* Excludes 39 people who were still studying, or who did not give enough information for classification, etc.

It is sometimes asserted, usually in polemic against the 'free' principle, that libraries discourage people from buying books. Ralph Harris, for example, complains of the unfairness to authors and publishers caused by 'the difficulty of selling to buyers in competition with uncharged borrowing. The increasing use of free public libraries has been accompanied by a steady fall in the domestic sales of bound books . . .'* The rights and wrongs of this dispute are not at present the point at issue, but the analytical implication is relevant: it is suggested that book buying and library membership are exclusive alternatives, or increasingly so. If this were true then it might at least help explain the absentee graduate.

The Young Publishers' survey found that 22 per cent of the people who borrowed books from libraries had bought a book within the last fortnight; that 58 per cent of all those who had bought a book within that period were library members, and that the 16 per cent of the members who had not bought a book for at least a year were themselves only 44 per cent of the larger group of all the people who had not bought a book in that time, all of which 'hardly suggests that libraries discourage book buying'. Our evidence points to the same conclusion, expressed for our purpose in the finding that library membership and book buying are not mutually exclusive alternatives; on the contrary, they are positively associated.

* Ralph Harris, in the introductory essay to A. P. Herbert's Hobart Paper, *Librarians: Free-for-All?*

| Table 24 | The sample: extent of book ownership | | | |
|---|---|---|---|---|
| | Members | Former | Non-members | Total |
| Number in sample | 160 | 144 | 197 | 501 |
| Number of books owned | Percentages | | | |
| 0 | 7 | 15 | 28 | 18 |
| 1–50 | 51 | 67 | 74 | 64 |
| 50–200 | 28 | 19 | 18 | 22 |
| 200+ | 21 | 14 | 8 | 14 |

There were several working class respondents who gave books away once they were read, and the complete breakdown on which Table 24 is based shows that, in 18 per cent of all households in this sample, there were said to be no books at all (which may mean only that the Bible or a home handyman's manual were simply taken for granted), and that these households were those of members, former members and non-members.* But whereas only seven per cent of the members said they had no books, 15 per cent of the former members and 28 per cent of the non-members had none. It is logically possible, of course, that people might buy *more* books if they could not borrow them for nothing; but it is clear that the people who do in fact buy books in fairly large numbers and those who belong to public libraries are by and large the same people.

There was one further way in which library members were compared with former and non-members: they were distinguished from each other by an 'index of intelligence'. This is not standard practice and it should therefore be briefly explained and justified. First, it seemed reasonable to expect that something like intelligence might be closely associated with library membership, and that, if it could be isolated, this factor might be more meaningful than, say, sheer length of education.† Secondly, it must be stressed that the method is an *index*, and not a *test* of intelligence, and it rests upon the discovery (by the BBC's Audience Research Department) that once an individual's occupational level and age are known, then it is possible to predict, with a high degree of accuracy,‡ to which of ten groups

* Cauter and Downham, in *The Communication of Ideas*, also noted that acquiring books is not so widespread among working class readers (who share books among themselves) as among middle class readers (who do not).

† The vague phrase 'something like intelligence' is used deliberately in conscious recognition of the known philosophical and scientific difficulties of this concept.

‡ A multiple correlation of +0·785 with intelligence defining 'intelligence' as *g* and assessed by the Vernon Abstraction Test.

in the population he belongs – ranging from the most intelligent ten per cent to the least intelligent ten per cent. Since education is one of the defining characteristics of the BBC's occupational scale, applying the index is a way of putting together three otherwise separate pieces of information about individuals.*

Table 25 The sample: library relationship by intelligence

| | Members | Former | Non-members | Total* |
|---|---|---|---|---|
| Number in sample | 148 | 135 | 191 | 474 |
| Intelligence group | Percentages | | | |
| I and II | 53 | 39 | 28 | 39 |
| III–VI | 30 | 36 | 36 | 35 |
| VII–X | 17 | 25 | 36 | 26 |

* Twenty-seven people were unclassifiable, for lack of one of the dimensions of the Index.

Table 25 shows that the index of intelligence markedly differentiates members from former members and non-members. (It also shows incidentally that this sample is overweighted with more intelligent and underweighted with less intelligent people.) It is especially striking that over half the members come from the two most intelligent tenths of the population, and that there are a disproportionate number of the least intelligent among the non-members. This does not, in itself, suggest a direction for library policy, which could arguably exploit the trend or resist it; but it does draw attention to a fact about the present relationship between libraries and their public which is likely to condition all attempts to develop or change that relationship.

There is a sense, then, in which the libraries' *clientèle* is middle-aged and middle class, but one of the objects of a survey of this kind is to expose the crudities of such generalisations. Major, even if not majority, sections of the libraries' public are young and working class. Even the index of intelligence, though a powerful distinguishing factor, cannot achieve a simple segregation between members and the rest.

This chapter has, however, outlined the differences, at a collective level, between members of public libraries and the population as a whole. The following three chapters record how the three dissimilar groups (those who belong to libraries, those who did once and those who never have) think about the public library service – not only in figures, but also in the words they actually used.

* See 'The Construction of an Index of Intelligence', W. A. Belson, in *Brit. Psych.*, Vol. XLVI, Part I, February 1955.

Chapter 6

# Public attitudes: (1) non-members

For any individual, there may be a host of reasons, some of them even hidden from himself, why he is or is not a member of a public library. At the level of statistical regularities at which this report – and librarians, as providers – must operate, it is clear that there are some factors which predispose people to become members, but that these are not all-powerful. People with little education join libraries, people with much do not. People of high intelligence let their membership lapse, while many with more modest capacities persist. Members were often encouraged by their schools, but non-members frequently resisted the message the schools were trying to convey to them. One must conclude that since the present limits to library use are not wholly set by nature, nor yet by other social institutions, they may partly be set by the libraries themselves – their resources and the way in which they are deployed.

It has already been noted that 'non-member' is not quite synonymous with 'non-user'. A few non-members use reading rooms and reference facilities. Their needs vary from the specialised to the everyday utilitarian – reading newspapers, looking at advertisements for jobs, seeing 'what's on at the pictures'. But the amount of such 'non-registered' use is slight among those who are not members. Reading books borrowed on other people's tickets is the main form that their non-registered use takes.

## Reasons for non-membership

The essential question is, then, why are non-members not members? Many people are likely to feel debarred because they are unable to read or are unused to reading, like the woman in Stoke Newington who described novels as 'the thick books with one story'. Illiteracy or near illiteracy creates strong feelings of shame in our society and consequently questions were put to non-members in ways that would spare them embarrassment on this account. This was partly a matter of the interviewers' approach, partly of presentation and wording. The issue was first broached obliquely: 'In fact, many people are like yourself – they don't belong to public libraries . . . why do you suppose this is?' Their spontaneous answers could be sorted into eight categories without undue distortion, and Table 26 shows the frequency with which these reasons were offered (some people gave more than one reason).

Table 26 Non-members' spontaneous reasons for not using libraries

| Reasons | Frequency of mention (per cent) |
|---|---|
| No time | 49 |
| No interest | 26 |
| Other activities preferred | 13 |
| Television | 11 |
| Other sources of books, reading material | 10 |
| Implied or explicit criticisms of library | 9 |
| Physical disabilities | 3 |
| Miscellaneous | 7 |

It will be appreciated that the object of the question was not to treat respondents as amateur sociologists, but to get them to evince their own attitudes, assuming that their answers were likely to be based on their own personal or immediate neighbourhood experience. 'No time' – the actual words were often used – usually carried with it the suggestion that the exigencies of life made it impossible to fit in reading, or even library visits. This reason is, therefore, not bracketed with the 'no interest/other activities preferred/television' group of answers, where the emphasis was more explicitly on personal preference. 'Television' (which might have headed the list, say, six years previously) stands either for distraction from reading because someone else has the set on, or for a positive preference for viewing rather than reading.

While Table 26 shows the incidence of different reasons for non-membership, the following quotations convey some of the individuality lost through merely counting heads.

*No time*

People haven't time and are too wrapped up in their own affairs. (*Shop assistant*)

Women go to work and, though better educated, don't have time to read. (*Assistant in dress shop*)

Probably dressmaking and knitting to do – these are my reasons. (*Shop assistant*)

*Not interested*

Some people can't read and some are not interested in books. (*Domestic worker*)

Reading is a minor entertainment compared with TV and pictures. (*Fitter and welder*)

You don't feel like reading if work in the office is boring. (*Cutter shopman*)

*Other sources of reading material*

Paper books are so cheap. (*Art dealer's receptionist*)

We are shocked at the small amount of reading active Christians do . . . I can get the latest books through a friend. (*Free Church minister*)

I'm happier with a newspaper or comic. (*Plumber and joiner*)

*Criticism of library*

Old books, worn out and torn. (*Ex-shop assistant*)

I think the same reason as me: you can get new books by subscription which you can't get at public libraries. (*Part-time secretary*)

I feel like an intruder in public libraries because of the atmosphere. A lot of people find this, I think. (*Typist-clerk*)

I've thought about joining but I read the reviews and I imagine it would be some time before one could get the book and by then we would have lost interest. (*Doctor's secretary*)

*Physical disabilities*

I get headaches if I read. (*Housewife*)

Reading makes me giddy. (*Joiner*)

I've never read much and now I'm past it. I'm 80 years old. (*Widow*)

These answers were all in response to an open-ended question. The limitation of such questions is that people cannot always muster their ideas during the interview. On the other hand, questions which present specific propositions may be misleading because they reflect the investigator's ideas of what might be important rather than the respondent's. In one situation, the respondent cannot always think quickly enough; in the other, his thinking is unduly directed. An attempt was made in this enquiry to mitigate these shortcomings by asking for spontaneous answers first in the manner described and then following up with: 'Here are other reasons which people sometimes give – do you think any of these are good reasons?' It is known that the order in which reasons are presented can influence replies, so interviewers were given cards with each reason shown separately, the sequence being changed at each interview. In addition to reporting comments, interviewers had also to record whether the person interviewed assented to the reason, rejected it, or had a mixed or neutral attitude towards it. These seven reasons were chosen because consultations with librarians, and the literature on library use, suggested that it would be fruitful to test the extent to which they are prevalent.

These were the reasons:

*A*. The books are dirty and unhygienic
*B*. The librarians make you feel uncomfortable
*C*. The building is a rather grim, official sort of place
*D*. It is difficult to get the kind of books I like
*E*. Reading books just doesn't interest me
*F*. Travelling to the library is awkward or expensive
*G*. I can't afford to belong to the library.

These reasons fall into two groups – lack of interest or involvement in the library's main stock-in-trade (*E*); and apprehensions about libraries (*A*, *B*, *C*, *D*, *G*), including difficulties experienced in travelling to them (*F*). The object was to determine the extent of support or rejection for each suggested reason and to discover which reasons apparently have the strongest deterrent effect.

Table 27 Attitudes to suggested reasons for non-membership

| Reasons | Endorsing Per cent | Rejecting Per cent | Mixed, neutral Per cent | |
|---|---|---|---|---|
| *A*. Unhygienic books | 11 | 71 | 18 | (100=195) |
| *B*. Starchy librarians | 7 | 67 | 26 | (100=194) |
| *C*. Grim building | 15 | 71 | 14 | (100=195) |
| *D*. Wrong books | 16 | 61 | 23 | (100=193) |
| *E*. Not interested | 43 | 40 | 17 | (100=195) |
| *F*. Travelling a bore | 14 | 78 | 8 | (100=193) |
| *G*. Cannot afford it | 2 | 88 | 10 | (100=192) |

*Indifference to reading*

Clearly, indifference to reading (*E*) is the most important reason why many people do not join libraries: they cannot read, they do not wish to read, or they are not able to give reading a higher priority in their lives. Nearly half the non-members fall into this group on both versions of the question (Tables 26 and 27). People seemed quite ready if necessary to identify themselves with reason (*E*) by making comments like: 'That's it really – that's like me.' Some were regretful:

I'm interested in reading, but I can't read – not newspapers either. (*A 22-year-old office cleaner*)

Others felt that their capacities were limited:

I suppose there are thousands like me – I begin a book and I can't finish it. (*Motor driver*)

I'm lost without a paper, but I can't settle to a book. (*Theatre musician*)

Or that their tastes or energy had changed with time:

I used to read novels a great deal when I was younger – used to buy those Collins sixpenny books as they came out – Dickens, *Green Gables*, *East Lynne*, but I don't seem interested in tales now. (*A 65-year-old shop assistant*)

I used to read myself silly – now just read newspapers and that's sufficient. (*Another shop assistant*)

Newspapers are not the only substitutes:

Not since the telly – prefer magazines, *True Romances* and those. (*Lorry driver's wife*)

I read all I want from the encyclopaedia – 16 volumes – I bought for the children. (*Antique dealer*)

Some people felt they would not be able to do all they must do if they were interested in reading as well:

If you've a couple of children you have no time for reading, especially if you can't get them to bed early – and I've had the decorating to do. (*Docker*)

My husband, he always has his nose in a book – nothing would get done if we were all the same. (*Housemaid*)

A small group suspected that reading was somewhat unhealthy or unnatural:

I suppose libraries are all right if you have nothing else to do. (*Swimming bath attendant*)

It doesn't seem normal to me to be always wanting to sit down and read a book. (*Housewife*)

These quotations are all from the non-members who did not read – 84 men and women out of 197. As many as 22 of these 84 were 66 years of age or more, 65 of them had left school at 15 or less, 65 owned fewer than 50 books or none at all, 53 believed that their schools had not encouraged them to be interested in public libraries, and 50 of them were in the bottom three occupational categories. It looks as if the hard core of indifference may be a passing problem for librarians and a fading reproach to the impoverished education systems of the past.

But non-readers account for only half the non-members. Others wholly dissociated themselves from this reason, like the hospital meals attendant who said: 'You can't be interested in anything if not in reading', or, as one housewife put it: 'There must be *some* reading that interests people, isn't there?'

## Apprehensions and misapprehensions

Apprehensions (or misapprehensions) about public libraries were much rarer than disinterest in reading. The purpose here was to discover whether anyone believed that library membership depended on direct payment of some kind of membership fee, whether the old fear that books might be contagious continued to persist, or whether people were deterred (justifiably or not) by the appearance of libraries, the manner of library staffs or the inadequacy of library stocks. There were a few non-members who were quite unable to answer these questions. A 26-year-old woman from Antigua, for instance, had never seen a library or a librarian. Nor had a 75-year-old bricklayer's widow in Finsbury, who did not know what a librarian was. For the most part, however, most non-members seem to come into contact with libraries (as voting stations, for example) or with library users (often their own children). Reading through their answers does not convey any sense that these respondents live in a world which is somehow insulated from all contact with libraries.

### *The cost of joining*

There were, however, a very small number of people who said that they could not afford to belong to a public library. Many of the ten per cent in the 'mixed, neutral' column (Table 27) did in fact believe that it costs something to join, but not enough to put them off, though some of these spoke as though fines were an inevitable concomitant of membership:

> No idea what it costs. (*Shopkeeper*)
>
> Don't think it costs much, about 2s 6d, I think. (*Ex-waitress*)
>
> It doesn't cost much – you might have to pay an entrance fee. (*Former GPO sorter*)
>
> It wouldn't bother me a bit – it just costs 6d or 1s to join. (*Docker*)
>
> Cost is the last thing in the world. What is it? Tanner a week? (*Housewife*)
>
> What for? Oh, that's if they're overdue – well, if you can't read a book in a month, you're a poor reader, aren't you? (*Cleaner*)

But 88 per cent of all non-members would agree, more or less, with the off-licence manager who said: 'Stupid, it's free!'

*Unhygienic books*

According to librarians fears that library books were insanitary used to be widespread. Such unjustified fears are no longer widespread, but neither are they extinct. The statement against which attitudes were tested (*A*) included the word 'dirty' as well as 'unhygienic', but some of the 11 per cent of the non-members (of all ages) who endorsed it clearly had contagiousness in mind:

> You don't know what homes those books have been in – there's people will read in the toilet – is that hygienic? I don't think so at all. (*Dress machinist*)
>
> I wouldn't take a borrowed book to bed – I'm slightly fussy. (*Translator*)
>
> You don't know who's handled them, do you? (*Counterhand*)

The feared hazards were not merely diseases:

> I've heard people say the books are dirty – egg and jam on books. (*Audit clerk*)

Some people adopted a tolerant approach, assuming that books are not hygienic while not blaming libraries:

> They can't help that. You can't expect them to buy books three or four times over. That's up to the people who borrow books. (*Retired doctor*)

To the great majority of people, a little grubbiness does not matter, or (and this view was frequently based on personal observation) they felt that the charge was without foundation:

> People that give this sort of reason are the same sort that in Communion object to drinking from the same chalice. (*Businessman*)
>
> That's bloody ridiculous, that is – that's an uncanny reason, that is. (*Butcher*)
>
> The books (my small daughter borrows) are all in good condition – beautiful books. (*Musician*)
>
> I've seen books here brought by the children and they are always lovely. (*Ex-home help*)

*Discouraging architecture*

Fifteen per cent of these non-members, nearly all of them under 45 years of age, thought that many public libraries looked unpleasant enough from the outside to discourage people from entering them: nearly as many accepted that they were often 'grim' to look at, but did not consider that an objection. But many more noted that libraries were improving in appearance. These contrasting remarks are typical of the main attitudes:

> What libraries I've seen look like a prison. (*Floorlayer*)

The type of building which looks like a law court – looks too officious. (*Design artist*)

Looks a bit official. (*Policeman*)

Has to be an official-looking place, it's a public library after all. (*Ex-telephonist*)

Now it's modern – different to what it was when I was a little girl. (*72-year-old labourer's widow*)

This library is so new and beautiful and all the books are new. (*Bookbinder*)

*The atmosphere and the staff*

A Stoke Newington housewife who used to be a nurse said: 'I haven't heard anybody say anything bad about librarians.' In fact, only seven per cent of all non-members thought that the demeanour of library staffs might discourage library membership. Complaints like this were extremely rare:

Yesterday I took my son's book back . . . rather pompous, but *young* lady . . . I went in to the exit, round table effort. She asked me to go out and come in the other door, instead of asking me to go round table . . . that is the sort of thing that would put my boy off going to the library altogether. (*Former nurse*)

A few non-members thought the atmosphere in public libraries discomforting ('staid' was the adjective one of them used), or that others might find it so:

I feel very uncomfortable in a library. I would be frightened they would come up to talk to me when picking out a book. If I'm shopping I don't like assistants round me. I like to relax and find for myself. (*Former home help*)

The sort of people who are put off by banks and administrative people might be put off. (*Advertising executive*)

Not all the several people who mentioned the atmosphere when asked about library staff were disturbed by it:

They are doing their job – you have got to be quiet. (*House painter*)

Not like a nightclub, but the people who use it are those who understand books. (*Housewife*)

Some who evidently came directly or indirectly into contact with librarians praised them in such terms:

I took some books back for the lady I worked for and they helped you all they could. (*Child minder*)

My girl's never complained. She quite likes it – and they show films and all one night a week. (*Van driver*)

There were a few comments that were, on the face of it, favourable to librarians or at least exonerating, but the approval seemed to stem from a disturbingly narrow conception of a librarian's role. For example:

> Some librarians may not be very nice, but it's just like going into a shop. You just go in and get a book. It doesn't matter what they're like . . . if you can't see the book you want, then you can ask them, and they'll tell you whether it's in or out . . . but I don't see how else they can help you. (*Ganger*)

It may not matter that one or two non-members speak like this, but it would be a point for serious consideration by the profession if their attitudes were to be shared by members and former members in significant numbers.

*The adequacy of book stocks*

'It is difficult to get the kind of books I like', turned out to be the second most important reason given for non-membership (16 per cent endorsed it and another 23 per cent did not reject it). Among the majority who did not accept this as a reason for not joining a public library were the tailor who said: 'Any book – they got it in a library', and the former machinst whose husband 'always gets the books he wants'. Another housewife said: 'My husband puts his name down, and they send him a card, if he wants a book they haven't got.' Different people will, however, evaluate the same experience in different terms:

> Ah, sometimes – I'm only going by cases I've heard – you have to wait – it's understandable, isn't it . . . my friends who I work with they put their name down on the list there to notify them by card. I've known them wait weeks for a particular book. (*Docker*)

Or they will judge in the light of modest expectations:

> They haven't got the books for everyone, but there is a good selection. (*Building labourer*)
>
> They supply every kind of book, unless you're one of those difficult people who tries to find something out of the ordinary. (*Butcher*)

Not everyone agrees with the glassworker who believed that: 'A library caters for everyone's taste.' A Chelsea film-winder, for example, said: 'I only like light adventure – nothing serious that you'd get out of the library.' And, by contrast, a policeman in the same borough explained: 'My interest in reading is to study, not novels.'

*Accessibility*

People were asked to react to the suggestion that travelling to the library is awkward or expensive; this was in effect a way of testing whether there are enough library service points within easy reach. Most non-members think that there is no cause for complaint: 'Not in London – there's no place too far; there's nearly one in every borough.' But there is a considerable minority, 14 per cent, who are themselves bothered by the cost or difficulty of getting to the library, or think that others may be:

They used to have a gentleman come round the streets and you just loaned the books from them. That would fall in line with people who say it's too far . . . but you don't see them here. People have got to go over the main road to the library. A lot of people would like a book to read but they get panicky crossing the road. (*Plumber*)

It's difficult to get to Church Street from here in bad weather – you'd have to change buses twice. (*Tobacconist*)

If I had a van coming round, I'd belong. (*Machinist*)

**Non-members and the prospect of joining**

From a librarian's point of view, two of the findings reported so far are particularly encouraging: first, those who seem not to be members because they are incapable of reading or indifferent to it are a vanishing minority. Secondly, although there are often many things that non-members do not know about public libraries, they do not inhabit a subculture in which all reference to libraries is lacking, or hostile. Not only did they know people who use public libraries and mostly accept this use as normal behaviour, but more than half of them (57 per cent) had been inside their local library building for one reason or another (to accompany a child member or to vote, for instance).

The proportion of those who have ventured into their libraries went up slightly more among men (61 per cent), among people in occupation groups 4–7 and those who liked school (both 60 per cent), and most of all among men and women aged 45 or more. Conversely, although 43 per cent of all non-members had not been inside their local library building for any reason, the proportion went up among women (46 per cent), those who had disliked school (48 per cent), those aged 15–45 years (49 per cent) or in the top three occupational groups (51 per cent). The biggest difference was found among those who left school younger than 15, of whom 56 per cent had not been inside their nearest library.

Those who said they had visited a library were asked how they felt about it. Some of the replies seemed genuinely favourable but inevitably some of them were perhaps little more than expressions of politeness:

Quite a nice place to spend an hour, if you have an hour to spare. (*Foreman painter*)

Very, very nice and very well cleaned and all. And a nice gentleman at the door and all. (*Plumber*)

The negative comments are less ambiguous:

It was just big; I didn't know where to start. (*21-year-old film winder*)

I had the usual feeling; it's grim, like a hospital or church, the 'County Council feeling'. (*Fitter welder*)

The interviews concluded (apart from 'personal data' questions) by asking all non-members whether they thought they might ever use a public library. The answers to such a question cannot, of course, be taken as a reliable guide to what people will actually do in the future, but they do offer further evidence of their attitudes. A majority of the non-members – 61 per cent – said explicitly or by implication that they thought they were likely to use the library at some time; the remaining 39 per cent did not expect to, and some of them were quite definite about it:

I won't. No; never. (*Lorry driver*)

I'd like to but it isn't much good if you can't read. (*Office cleaner*)

I don't think I would become a member – haven't the time, see, now I'm courting. (*Butcher*)

There's no good saying 'yes', when I mean 'no'. (*Counterhand*)

No: I get halfway through the *Mirror* and that's my lot. (*Another cleaner*)

Some of those in the positive 61 per cent sounded almost as sure:

When I retire from work I shall, very definitely. (*Industrial caterer*)

When the family are off my hands and I can sit down of an afternoon. (*Housewife*)

But there are, of course, many reasons, personal and circumstantial, why these expressions of intention could lead to nothing; and statements, though sincere, may be as poorly predictive as those of Pinter's Caretaker perpetually meaning to get his papers from Sidcup:

In future years, when I'm a grandma. I've often felt I'd like to join, when I've heard about books on 'Woman's Hour'. (*Housewife*)

I think I'd like to borrow language records and perhaps books. (*Head-waiter*)

I would use reference books which would help me – languages, for instance. (*Clergyman*)

Though nothing can be predicted about future behaviour, it can be said that three in every five non-members have a favourable attitude towards public libraries, and many of them have a sense, in some detail, of the use they could make of a library's resources. This well-disposed majority of 61 per cent rises considerably (to 75 per cent) for people who left school after 15, and by several degrees among the top three occupational categories, the under-45s, and those who liked being at school.

It is clear that, though many people do not belong to public libraries because they are poor readers or indifferent to books, to many others there is at least the prospect of joining, and it is not distasteful, except perhaps to the stoical woman who said she might join because 'You never do know what might be in store for you'.

Chapter 7

# Public attitudes: (2) former members

The previous chapter presented a profile of the kind of person who does not belong to a public library. The purpose of this chapter is to give a comparable picture of those who used to be public library members but who have let their membership lapse. This is obviously a particularly interesting, possibly crucial group of people, both for a study of the effectiveness of relations between public libraries and the public, and, in practice, for those who aim to provide an attractive library service.

In the same way that 'non-member' is not quite synonymous with 'non-user', 'former member' is not quite synonymous with 'former user'. Former members can still make use of reference and reading room facilities though, of course, they cannot borrow books or records except on someone else's ticket. One-fifth of the former members reported that they read books taken out on other members' tickets but this does not necessarily imply that they went to the library themselves to borrow such books. Some of the women who were once members occasionally changed books for other members of the family.

Librarians who are anxious about 'turnover' may endure a refinement to their concern: are former members lapsed temporarily or lost for ever? Is non-membership a passing phase for former members or is it a real break with the library service? Over three-quarters of the former members had let their membership lapse for four or more years at the time of the survey. Over a third had let their membership lapse for ten years or more. Though many said in reply to a direct question (similar to the one put to non-members) that they might use the library in the future (111 or 78 per cent) the length of time that had passed since a majority had been members, implies that it would be unwise to take this intention too seriously. The seven per cent whose membership had lapsed for less than a year at the time of the survey might well become members again, providing they are not discouraged:

> Only because I have moved, I plan to join again. I have been to the library but they said I had to show my rent book to show I lived here. (*Nurse orderly*)

Many of the others must be regarded as having permanently joined the ranks of non-members, and there was, of course, a time when it was less than a year since *their* membership had lapsed.

## Reasons for lapsed membership

At some time all the former members had been attracted into registered membership. What, then, had made them withdraw from active use of their libraries facilities? Was it something about the libraries or about themselves? Asked by interviewers almost casually, 'Can you recall why you gave up belonging to the library?', some were genuinely stumped by the question, like the retired domestic help who said: 'No reason. Just faded out of using it.' Most of the spontaneous reasons given could be grouped into ten categories. As with non-members there were people who had no time, lacked interest, or said there were other things they liked better; who borrowed books in other ways, or bought cheap editions. There were people who had moved from one district to another, and, finally, there was a small group which explicitly linked leaving school and going out to work with leaving the library. Some people gave more than one reason and these have been counted under the heading which seemed to correspond with the most salient reason. Thus 'lack of time – moved from the district' was classified as 'moved' where other replies in the course of the interview indicated that the move had broken the habits of the family for a time. Table 28 shows the frequency with which such reasons were offered.

Table 28 Spontaneous reasons for leaving library (former members)

| Reasons | Frequency of mention (per cent) |
|---|---|
| No time | 31 |
| Moved from the district | 18 |
| Criticism of libraries | 11 |
| Other sources of books | 6 |
| Other activities preferred | 6 |
| Left school | 6 |
| Physical disability | 6 |
| Lack of interest | 6 |
| Cheaper books | 4 |
| Television | 3 |
| Others | 5 |

Nearly a third of the former members, then, offered 'no time' as a reason. The only other reason given by any sizeable group was 'moved from the district'. Comments in some way critical of public libraries were made, however, by over one in ten of the sample, and six per cent of these former members recalled that leaving school was the occasion of letting their membership lapse.

'No time' could be a rationalisation masking more pertinent reasons for breaking the library habit. To get beyond the phrases that come to mind most easily, respondents were shown a list of reasons why other people gave up being library members, and asked to say if these statements corresponded with or were close to their own reasons. These were the reasons offered:

*A.* I moved to a new district and broke the habit
*B.* I finished exams/gave up studying
*C.* I preferred doing other things to reading books
*D.* I prefer buying my own books
*E.* I couldn't get the books I wanted
*F.* The library opens at awkward hours
*G.* My eyesight wasn't good enough (or other disability)
*H.* I didn't like the atmosphere in the library
*I.* I didn't get on with a member of the staff
*J.* I found the rules and/or fines a nuisance
*K.* The library was awkward/expensive to get to
*L.* I gave it up when I got married/started a family.

These reasons, like those presented to non-members, fall into two main groups, one relating to the service offered by the library (*E, F, H, I, J, K*) and the other, directly or indirectly, to changes in the person's habits or circumstances (*A, B, C, D, G, L*). The following table (Table 29) shows the importance attributed by former members to each of the listed reasons.

Table 29 Percentage agreement with suggested reasons for giving up library membership (former members)

| 'Personal' reasons | Per cent | 'Library' reasons | Per cent |
|---|---|---|---|
| Moved | 42 | Could not get books | 16 |
| Other activities preferred | 34 | Rules or fines | 10 |
| Marriage, etc. | 27 | Atmosphere | 8 |
| Prefer to buy | 26 | Inconvenient hours | 8 |
| Eyesight, etc. | 13 | Travelling awkward, etc. | 7 |
| Gave up studying, etc. | 9 | Staff | 4 |

**Personal factors**

*I moved . . . and broke the habit*

When actually presented with a list of possible reasons for giving up library membership, more agreed with the statement 'I moved to a new district and broke the habit' than any of the other reasons suggested to them. This finding indicates that moving may be the *precipitating* cause of the failure to renew library membership and though many may *intend* to rejoin they just never get round to it:

> Moved into a new business. (*Newsagent*)
>
> Because we moved down here, with every intention of rejoining, but too busy getting house straight for the moment. (*Sales office manager*)
>
> Because I was intending all the time to leave the country and I figured that after I'd settled down in the (new) country I could join one. (*Diesel motor mechanic*)

Some library users seem to become attached to a particular library rather than to libraries in general. Once they have joined and borrowed a book then the obligation to return it makes them go back to the library again, and so exposes them to the attraction or temptation of taking out another book. But when the cycle is broken by moving, continuity is lost and the effort of rejoining is too great:

> We moved out of the district. The library was not so near from up there. It was too much trouble. Being a young boy I used to go to the play centre, the youth club. I did other things. (*Floor-layer*)

Moving, especially from one district to another, is commonly caused by other major changes in life, and sometimes these were mentioned in their own right. But any kind of disruption – the loss of a husband or wife, a change of job or getting into the services, can break the library habit.

> I think in 1943–44. I joined the ATC [Air Training Corps] then it lapsed – book reading became left behind and I have never since been there. (*Assistant operations manager*)
>
> The First World War – everything went haywire or closed down. (*Hospital and school cook*)

For some, leaving school was just such a disruption:

> Really you know, I've never been one for reading books. Once I left school I started to go out dancing and one thing and another. (*25-year-old accounting machine operator*)
>
> I suppose I left school and maybe when young . . . a phase of reading, and then it wore off. (*35-year-old delivery-van driver*)
>
> I just automatically finished going there, leaving school and going to work. (*49-year-old lorry driver*)

'No time', 'TV watching', 'lack of interest', 'other activities' and 'physical disabilities' were given spontaneously as reasons for lapsed membership by just over half the former members. Various though these reasons are, there is a common factor of change underlying many, though not of course all of them.

> I have moved – and now have less time. Keeping my flat up and my garden. (*Civil service clerical officer*)
>
> In 1957 I went into hospital for two months for correction of a squint, had to give up reading for a time. (*Housewife, former machinist*)
>
> I had too much to do – babies and one thing and another. (*Another housewife, also a former machinist*)

When the reasons spontaneously given for discontinuing library membership are considered in the light of this basic element of major change – occupation, leaving school, going abroad, developing a physical handicap, having a large family, as well as the more direct factor of changing residence – then about half of all the explanations given refer to some kind of break in the person's way of life. It is impossible to *prove* on the basis of the material collected in this survey that it is this element of disruption that causes the break in library membership, but a higher proportion of former members (ten per cent against four per cent of members) were new to the addresses where they were interviewed. The relations between changes, either voluntary (like moving house) or involuntary (like going blind), and library membership would repay further enquiry. It looks as though former members are men and women who have some interest in books and libraries, but the link is easily broken.

*Other activities preferred*

Though moving and other kinds of change may have caused the break, other factors tend to confirm former members in their non-membership. Reasons classifiable as 'other activities' were only mentioned spontaneously by a few people, but when presented with the list of possible causes, over a third of them agreed with 'I preferred doing other things to reading books'. Television, mentioned by a barmaid as 'a counter-attraction', and spontaneously by only three per cent of the sample, did not predominate in the replies.

> I just lost interest, took more interest in dancing and such. Packed it up rather suddenly. (*Domestic help*)

There is little or no real sense of loss. Activities other than reading take up so much time and are evidently so interesting that reading is not missed. The replies evoke a positive picture of what activities these people care about, so that they are much less the apparently negative creatures categorised by the term 'former members':

I joined the church choir and that sort of thing, and the Church Lads' Brigade. (*Retired railway coppersmith*)

Going to the pictures, and to youth clubs to play table tennis and snooker. (*17-year-old painter's labourer*)

I played a lot of sport – I play golf regularly now. (*Keg manufacturer's guillotine and press operator*)

Knitting is perhaps the most unremarked addiction of British women, and there were several in this sample who preferred it:*

I'd sooner knit than read. (*27-year-old assistant in a chemist's shop*)

Well, you have other things to do – with a family growing up there's always something to do, and I like knitting and sewing. (*Housewife*)

I felt by knitting I had something to show for it. (*Accounting machine operator*)

As had this medical research worker: 'I preferred pottery and art classes – not the time for reading.' Reading, for some, is literally unproductive, a waste of time. For a few, the antithesis is even more fundamental:

You know when you get away from school you have a kind of fondness for life for a little while. (*Self-employed builder*)

Perhaps the same contrast – life versus the book – was implied by the now middle-aged tropical helmet machinist who said: 'I think it's more for older people to go in there. . . .'

*Marriage*

For some, it was not, or not only, such alternative enthusiasms, but the responsibilities of marriage and children that had led to their not being members:

I just didn't find the time to read, not when you had youngsters and a husband out of the Army. I was occupied. (*Machinist*)

Hadn't got time. Having a baby. I gave up my job (night-nursing) and didn't need to read so much. (*SRN*)

Men were just as likely as women to say that marriage was part of their reason for not being library members any longer:

Only because I moved from the district and became a householder and father and don't have much reading time. (*Bank clerk*)

I think the main reason is that most people don't have time. There's no quiet because of young children: only one living-room. (*Gas-meter reader*)

* Cauter and Downham found in their Derby survey that for 37 per cent of the women interviewed knitting was the most popular activity and for 32 per cent needlework was the favourite. The findings of *Education and Retirement* were similar.

People like to be by themselves or quiet when they read and in some homes the family is felt to be an uncongenial background for reading.

*Buying books preferred*

Though, as has already been shown, buying books does not inhibit library membership, a quarter of the former members did say that they preferred to buy books rather than borrow them from the library. Nearly half of these had over a hundred books of their own while only a small fraction of the rest owned as many as a hundred. It looks as if a strong preference for buying books helps a section of the former members to continue in their non-membership:

> Got enough books of my own. I became a book collector of my own. Friends gave me a lot. Two other friends who died left me their books. I've got my own library now. (*Postman*)

There is almost a sense of pride in the ability to do without the library service:

> Because I started buying my books. I only belong to the American Embassy library because I cannot buy those books here. (*Electronic engineer*)

Library membership, for some, belonged to the days when books were too expensive for them or when they had little money to spare:

> Now I buy my own books but I couldn't afford it in the old days. (*Business executive*)

For a few, buying books marked them off not from past poverty but from other people:

> In my range of experience people don't buy books although I prefer to buy my books when I have read the reviews. (*Bank clerk*)

The technical nature of the books some respondents required tended to make them turn to sources other than the public library. In this sense, statements about buying rather than borrowing could be classified with the other group of statements – those (not always accurate) statements about library provision:

> Yes, I found other sources of supply for what I wanted. The sort I want are firmly trade books, a closely reasoned and informative run-down on modern rubber planting for instance. It is next door to impossible to get a thesis on the requisition of property. . . . If the libraries would *take* these sort of things. . . . (*Ex-property dealer*)
>
> Most of the books I have, I've had to buy – on dairying and chemistry. The firm I worked for got them at half price for us. (*Proprietor of a small dairy*)

It seems that some people who are interested only in technical works assume that they place themselves outside the range of the library service, or consider that it could not help them.

*Giving up studying*

Though leaving school or giving up studying figured on a small scale in the spontaneous reasons for giving up library membership, some nine per cent did agree that these events were associated with their discontinuing:

> I gave up studying. I took up another form of studying – police work – which the library couldn't cater for because it's confidential. (*Police constable*)
>
> Because I finished reading and studying the books. (*Tailor's cutter*)
>
> In a way – like when I was breeding budgerigars – I read all the books there were about budgerigars. (*Sewing machine mechanic*)
>
> Yes, to some extent, I finished my apprenticeship. I need it only now to settle an argument on a technical point. (*Press tool maker*)

Thus a minority of former members connected the library with 'study' rather than with 'recreational' forms of reading, so that once they had finished studying they automatically gave up using the library.

*Physical disabilities*

A small minority, mostly of people aged 56 or more, spontaneously gave such reasons as 'blindness' or 'infirmity' for their lapse in library membership, though books in Braille are obtainable through London libraries. When presented with the check list of possible reasons, rather more agreed that poor eyesight or some other handicap was related to their discontinuing library membership:

> I'm under the hospital. They say I mustn't use my eyes much. (*Grocer*)
>
> I lost my sight and had to use Braille books. (*Piano tuner*)
>
> My eyes are not so good at night. (*Supervisor*)

At least six per cent of former members were deterred by physical disabilities, and probably an extra seven per cent felt that their handicaps made visits to the library difficult or dangerous ('it's the steps').

**Dissatisfaction with the library service**

When people were asked what made them give up being library members, their replies more often referred to themselves than to libraries. It is consistent with this, and with the 'personal crisis' explanation offered so far, that former members do not seem to have had more tenuous relationships with the library than those of members. In the first place, on their own reporting, former members seem to have used the library as frequently as present members. The fact that frequency of use between members and former members is not significantly different gives some further support to the idea that a distinct change in habits led to a more or less sharp break with the library for a good proportion of former members.

Table 30 Frequency of library use (members and former members)

| | Members | | Former members | | Total | |
|---|---|---|---|---|---|---|
| | Number | Per cent | Number | Per cent | Number | Per cent |
| At least monthly | 133 | 83 | 109 | 77 | 242 | 81 |
| At longer intervals | 27 | 17 | 35 | 23 | 62 | 19 |
| | 160 | 100 | 144 | 100 | 304 | 100 |

In the second place, former members were just as likely as members to have borrowed books from the library, and to have used the reading room and made use of other services, with two exceptions. They were slightly less likely to have used the library for reference purposes – a use which perhaps reinforces membership – and much less likely to have borrowed gramophone records.

Table 31 Type of use made of library (former members and members)

| | Former members | | Members | | Total | |
|---|---|---|---|---|---|---|
| | Number | Per cent | Number | Per cent | Number | Per cent |
| Borrowing books | 144 | 100 | 157 | 98 | 301 | 99 |
| Reference | 57 | 40 | 82 | 51 | 139 | 46 |
| Newspapers | 30 | 21 | 39 | 24 | 69 | 23 |
| Records | 4 | 3 | 18 | 11 | 22 | 7 |
| Other | 19 | 13 | 15 | 9 | 34 | 11 |

The latter finding is probably due mainly to the length of time that had elapsed since most of them had been members – ten years and more for over a third of them; that is, for many of them, before the establishment of gramophone record libraries. Apart from these two facilities, then, there was little difference in frequency or type of use between those who now are and those who used to be members.

Eleven per cent of the former members, when giving spontaneous reasons for their discontinued membership, did however criticise the library service. Remarks that could be interpreted as critical of the service included those – and there were many of them – caused by distance from a library, rather than deficiencies in what it offered.

Well it was inconvenient to get there. (*Motorman on the Underground*)

The little shop near where I work is near and more convenient. (*Canteen assistant*)

I moved and had such a lot of work to get the flat ready – and the new library here is just off my usual route. Get most of the books we want in Penguins. (*Buyer for clothing store*)

One cannot assume that people who *buy* books do so because they cannot get them at the library, but in some cases replies indicating a preference for buying books or implying their easier availability from our sources can be taken as criticisms of the library service. Going to the library is, in short, a bother, especially when books can be bought or there are readier sources of supply:

The only reason is I don't pass it – if I do I'm in a hurry. If I didn't have an alternative I'd be a member. (*Postman on shift work*)

I moved from the district – I've other interests now I'm older. I think you have to be really interested and want a bit of a read before you get on a bus and go down there to the library. Too far just to look at the papers. People can afford papers nowadays. (*Old Age Pensioner*)

We gave up when we moved and now our tickets have expired. My daughter of 13 doesn't bother as they have a good library at [her] comprehensive school. (*Housewife*)

Nevertheless, even the supply, in a sense, of a list of possible grievances with the library service did not release a flood of criticism as Table 29 shows. The most important sources of dissatisfaction are indicated by the frequency with which the former members agreed with the six critical items: from the 16 per cent who complained that they could not borrow the books they wanted to the small group who criticised the staff.

*Could not get books*

The difficulty which people have experienced in obtaining books, or the time lag before recently published books or books in great demand are available, is the most important source of dissatisfaction with the service.

You'd hear about a book and you'd ask. It wouldn't be in. Have to reserve it and have to wait. (*Post Office sorter*)

Some are critical only of the specific library not of the service in general.

I went to another branch when I couldn't get the books – it had a better selection. (*Assistant operations manager*)

Some felt the library had no more to offer them.

As I say – there is no more in the library on my interest. (*Sewing machine mechanic*)

Libraries were criticised both for not having popular works easily available and for not keeping up to date with technical literature.

I don't think they keep up to date with modern technical books such as photography, and even if they do they don't get enough copies. (*Civil Service research officer*)

This feeling that the right books are hard to come by obviously predisposes a small minority to look elsewhere. On the other hand, most of the former members did not leave for this reason and some were enthusiastic about the help they had received in getting books.

*Fines and rules*

Fines were without a doubt part of the explanation for the withdrawal of some people from library membership:

Fines were a nuisance. (*Assistant operations manager*)

I got interested in geography so I went along and joined but I got fined so much I gave it up. (*Laboratory assistant*)

Others thought fines were 'a good thing' and that if 'you can't read a book in a fortnight you deserve to be fined'. One respondent said directly that some people ought to be 'deterred' from the library. Most would have agreed with the man who said 'I'd pay up and forget.' But whether respondents agreed with the existence of fines and regulations or not, a minority had been effectively 'deterred' out of membership by them.

*Atmosphere and staff*

The atmosphere in the library ranked third in this group of sources of dissatisfaction:

Never did like it, like a morgue, daren't say a word, working clothes and boots are heavy, they make a noise, people wonder what you are. (*Lathe turner*)

They are cold looking aren't they? They just got a funny cold atmosphere like you have to watch yourself and be quiet. They [the staff] look a bit up in the air, don't they? I suppose they looked unpleasant to me then. I only asked them where the books was and they just told you. They're just like old maids: they are, mostly, aren't they? They don't say nothing. (*19-year-old delivery man*)

Criticisms about staff were, in fact, only made by four per cent of former members.

Some will help no end, others could not care less, but not very often, not enough to put *me* off, but I noticed it. (*Piano tuner*)

The feeling was sometimes expressed that the approach should come from the library staff rather than that the library user should make his needs known:

You were never able to get the books you wanted. I didn't ask for them to get them. I never bothered them. They just didn't seem to bother with you so you didn't bother with them. If the books were there, you took them, if not you didn't. (*Self-employed – television sales and service*)

*Inconvenient hours and travelling*

The inconvenience of hours and difficulties associated with travelling were more clearly brought out in response to the prompted question though again they related only to a minority. Men were more likely to mention awkward hours than women:

The hours are awkward, but I don't finish work till 11 at night. About one o'clock in the morning would suit me! (*Television sales*)

Prefer longer hours. They close too early in London. In Glasgow the library stays open until 9.30. (*Trainee Customs and Excise officer*)

That [the hours] would be a reason as well, you see, not getting home till 7.30. (*Retired coppersmith*)

The inconvenience of travelling is probably more important than the cost:

It is a bit awkward to get to, a long walk. (*Bank clerk*)

No, where I was I didn't have to pay for it. I had to walk. (*Housewife, former machinist*)

If the library were nearer, say on my way home, I would call in. (*Civil Service executive officer*)

Some respondents spoke as though they were limited by their working hours, even when they were normal, rather than by the opening hours of the library. This illustrates the deferential tone that frequently affects talk about public libraries. Because of this deference respondents were asked: 'why do you suppose many people don't use the public library service'? It was thought that respondents might be more willing to attribute critical attitudes to other people than they would be to admit such attitudes themselves. The following table (Table 32) shows that this is indeed so.

Table 32 Members' reasons for other peoples' failure to use libraries

| Reasons | Number | Per cent |
|---|---|---|
| Television | 64 | 50 |
| Lack of interest | 40 | 31 |
| Criticism of libraries | 32 | 25 |
| Other activities preferred | 27 | 21 |
| No time | 26 | 20 |
| Cheaper books | 15 | 12 |
| Others | 7 | 6 |

*N.B.*—Only 128 former members gave reasons.

When Table 31 is compared with Tables 29 and 30, lack of interest is said to affect other people by 31 per cent of the former members against only six per cent of the respondents themselves. Other people are much more likely to be watching television (50 per cent think so) than the people interviewed (three per cent), but, interestingly, other people are also slightly more likely to be buying cheap editions. The respondents were consistent, and regarded lack of time as less of a problem for the others than for themselves.

It is impossible to say to what extent the former members were projecting their own attitudes through these opinions about people in general, or to what extent they were merely uttering received ideas, but Table 31 probably indicates the direction in which their observations about themselves should be interpreted.

**Improvements to the service**

Former members were asked whether there was some service they thought the local library should offer but does not. Over half said 'no' to this question, sometimes implying that they thought the service was satisfactory, like the centre lathe turner who said: 'It is basically a public lending library and it does that.' Another one in five did not know what to say, leaving a third with specific improvements to suggest. Two-thirds of those making suggestions said they would join the library again if such services were provided. It is hardly possible to classify the kinds of improvement desired in any meaningful sub-groups but a selection from what the respondents had to say will illustrate some of the perceived or presumed deficiencies of the service:

> You should be allowed to use the library in another borough. (*Press operator*)
>
> There is something I would like – I do know of other boroughs that lay on a van system. My mother would welcome that. There must be other Old Age Pensioners who would like it too. (*Postman*)
>
> It's only my own opinion of course. I know it wouldn't work out but they should get in some pop-music records. They only ever have the old-time music you know an' that. I don't like that. (*Butcher*)

Some suggestions implied that library buildings are isolated and should be incorporated into some kind of civic or social centre:

> I think the library should blend with the activities of the borough. For example, ten-pin bowling, which is a new sport, should be connected with the public library. (*A man connected with ten-pin bowling*)

Another indication of the social centre idea:

> They could serve tea. (*Die casting engineer*)

Some implied that the existing services should be improved:

> When you put sixpence down on a book you never get it. Just nothing and that's very bad. (*Tailor's cutter*)
>
> Well there's only one thing. In some smaller libraries some of their reference books aren't up to date. They should try and keep up to date. (*Newsagent*)
>
> I think they should have more trade books on modern things. (*Laboratory assistant*)

Many former members did not, however, seem to be particularly concerned about the deficiencies of the service. Their library membership was a thing of the past, something they had grown out of, something they sometimes regretted slightly but not enough to take time from their family, their work or other more demanding or more attractive calls on their time.

Chapter 8

# Public attitudes: (3) members

The previous chapter found that the withdrawal of former members from library membership was not markedly related to feelings that the service was inadequate. It seemed to be connected more with major changes that had taken place, such as moving or leaving school, and that had broken the library habit. Despite good intentions, membership was subsequently not renewed. For others the day to day exigencies of family and work left little or no time for reading and other interests more directly bound up with the family or work had taken its place.

Turning to those who were at the time of the survey registered members of public libraries, it has already been shown that members know more about the services the libraries offer than the former members or non-members do, though there are some notable gaps even in their knowledge.

Members were more likely, as noted in the previous chapter, to make use of reference facilities and to borrow gramophone records than were former members, though the frequency with which the two groups used or formerly used the library is not significantly different. However, not all members did use the library frequently and a distinction can be made between the 80 per cent of *effective members* (i.e. those that use the library at least once a month) and *non-effective members* (i.e. those who use the library at less frequent intervals than once monthly). Of the effective members a third go to the library at least weekly and might be said to make intensive use of the service: they are men and women in equal proportions. The finding that such a high proportion of members use the library at frequent intervals again helps to confirm the hypothesis that for the majority of former members the break with the library habit was probably sudden. People seem on the whole either to use the library service regularly or not at all. There are very few who remain as registered members without borrowing books or using the reference library at regular, close intervals.

The intensiveness with which members use the library service would seem to indicate that they are by and large satisfied with it, although even on this scale they could be using it in spite of its shortcomings. To discover what in fact they do think of the service members were asked about these aspects of the library service: the availability of books, records and reference information; cataloguing; the system of returning and renewal operated by the libraries; and the facilities for reserving books and obtaining material from other libraries. They were also asked about the library staff and about selected physical attributes of the library buildings (Tables 33(a), 33(b) and 34). Finally (Table 35), they were asked to compare certain public services, the library service included, by ranking them on a five-point scale.

Table 33(a) Extent of members' satisfaction with the borrowing system and cataloguing

| | Satisfied (per cent) | Not satisfied (per cent) |
|---|---|---|
| Returning books | 95 | 5 |
| Renewing loans | 95 | 5 |
| Rules | 99 | 1 |
| Reservations | 98 | 2 |
| Cataloguing* | 75 | 12 |

* No firm opinion was expressed by 13 per cent.

Table 33(b) Degree of members' satisfaction with the service provided

| | Well satisfied (per cent) | Fairly satisfied (per cent) | Not satisfied (per cent) |
|---|---|---|---|
| Getting books wanted | 67 | 22 | 11 |
| Getting reference information | 83 | 13 | 4 |
| Staff | 83 | 13 | 4 |

## Availability of books

Perhaps the most obvious, because the most central, source of dissatisfaction with public libraries would be their inability to meet demands for particular kinds of books. Members were asked: 'Do you find it easy to get the kind of books you want? 'Ease' would depend, basically, on three factors – the adequacy of the stock, the intelligibility of its display, and access to the stock of other libraries. Two-thirds of the members replied affirmatively to this question.

Well, there's always enough books there. (*Waiter*)

They keep a wide selection. (*Electrical contractor*)

No trouble at all, the books are well displayed, you can see at a glance. (*Retired serving maid*)

Oh yes, I read crime books. (*Widow*)

Some of these respondents qualified their replies in ways which indicated that there were limits to the availability of books; they were not always available on the spot and reservations sometimes had to be made or other books obtained from elsewhere. These limits were not always felt as defects in the system:

Yes, only I had to wait. (*School cleaner*)

If the book that I want is not there they let me know when it's in. (*Tailor*)

If they haven't got it they get it from another branch or another library altogether. (*Trainee quantity surveyor*)

Others found that specific types of books were difficult to come by:

I've never had any difficulty with fiction but non-fiction is more awkward. I went to France and couldn't get any non-fiction on it. (*Teacher*)

Broadly speaking, yes, but they don't always have the specialised music books I want. (*Professional musician*)

For some people, 'ease' depended on when they went to the library. A depot inspector commended this ruse: 'If you go towards the time when people have taken back their books (6–6.30 pm) there are plenty of books in. Good books don't stay on the shelves very long.' The inability of the library to meet specialist or other kinds of demand either quickly or at all is accepted by some people as inevitable. Such limitations do not make them critical of the service in general. Other library users are more overtly critical. A fifth of the members felt that it was only 'fairly easy' to get the books they required.

Fairly easy. I am not hard to please – novels and amateur gardening mainly. My husband sometimes goes to the Central library to get photography books. (*Clerk*)

With patience. It's looking for a certain author that you've made up your mind to read that takes time – not always in. (*Retired post office sorter*)

The remark 'I'm not hard to please', which several people made, may imply that the deficiencies of the service in obtaining specific books are greater than they recognise. A few were a little more precise in their criticisms:

I couldn't get a book on the fishing industry and I asked three of the staff there who couldn't find anything on the subject. (*Student*)

If you are reading fiction and blood-and-thunders I think you can get them easily. If you want heavier reading it's not so easy. Perhaps they don't think people want that type of book. One book took nearly three months to get. (*Shorthand typist*)

Many of the criticisms were directed at branch libraries rather than at the service in general.

There are limitations on the variety and amount of books for a branch library. (*Stock cutter*)

Sometimes I use other libraries for specialised books. (*Freelance stage designer*)

Finally, another one in ten of the members said they did not find it easy to get the books they wanted, especially at branch libraries.

Not (easy) in branch. It's easier in the main. The facilities could be improved in the branch. Wider choice and the ability to reserve books without a long wait, without palaver and cost – sixpence for each special book. Puts it out of reach for poorer people. (*Senior Government official*)

Not the kind of books I like. You know what I mean – it's mostly all romantic stuff over there. Apart from reading westerns and a good gangster book, I'm very interested in football, like Danny Blanchflower's book. There's nothing like that over there. Not the latest books. (*Dustman*)

The comment of the Government official brings out well the attitude of a small group who feel that if the library sets out to provide an adequate service the consumer should not have to *pay* because he wants an unusual book or because a book is in great demand. The dustman was not alone in implying that he had cut down his use of the library because he could not obtain the books he wanted.

It was not, as we have said, the purpose of the enquiry to compare one borough with another, but it should perhaps be recorded that the number who found it easy to get the books they required outnumbered those who had some difficulty in all seven areas. It may have been a sampling fluke that made the service at Stoke Newington attract fewer than its share of criticisms on this score.

**Availability of gramophone records**

As noted earlier the proportion of members who borrow records from the library is extremely small—11 per cent of this sample. Not everyone has a gramophone, but part of the reason for this low proportion may be that record borrowing facilities are not available in all branches, though they are provided by all the library services in the survey. There may be many therefore who feel with the respondent who said 'I would if I could'. Of the 18 record borrowers, six said they could get the type of records they wanted and 11 either could not get what they wanted or found some difficulty in so doing.

For the number of people who borrow it's too small a stock. Hampstead has a very high percentage of borrowers. You can get them ultimately but I'm too mean to put in a request form. You have to pay sixpence to reserve a work. The records are in a bad state. (*Professional musician*)

I can't get the records. What few things there are are out. I ask them to reserve them for me. *Carmen* – I had to reserve that. *Tosca* – I had to reserve that. Four different operas I asked for I had to reserve every one. I didn't know there were so many lovers of opera in Stepney. I don't blame the library but most records you get are scratched through mishandling them. (*Dustman for the City of London*)

Usually out and I have to wait. I reserve them if I really want them but I don't use it very often. (*Engineer*)

What I want is always out. You have to take your pick from what's left, not what you want. The condition of the records is fairly good but people play them on poor machines with blunt needles. There's lots of surface noise. I change my stylus after every 100 sides and if I play these bad records on my machine it will spoil my stylus and my own records. (*Manager of reproduction department, printing trade*)

I don't find it easy. I know they are there but someone else has always got them. (*Housewife, former teacher*)

First of all, then, records are said not always to be available. Secondly, when they are available the selection is limited and the potential user has to be prepared to pay for reserving records. And thirdly, the records may be in a bad condition. Record-lending may be a minority service but if the comments of the record borrowers in this survey are representative it is, at the moment, not bringing a high degree of contentment to them.

**Ease of obtaining reference information**

Just under half the members use the reference library and two-thirds of these are men (so there is some basis for Mr Gerard's question – why don't women use the reference library?). Members who did use the reference facilities were asked whether they found it easy to get the kind of reference information they wanted. A large majority said that it was (see Table 33(b)). Several were positively complimentary:

Never been dissatisfied yet. (*Civilian police driver*)

They are very helpful over there. (*Labourer*)

One only has to enquire to be told where the books are. (*Designer in advertising*)

Again branch libraries were not felt or expected to be as adequate as the central library:

> If I want information which they can't get, they ring through to the central library. (*Stock cutter*)
>
> Main, yes, excellent. Average in branch library. (*Government official*)

Naturally some kinds of information tax a library's resources more than others:

> On the last two occasions information hasn't been in a book in the library. (*Constructional engineer*)
>
> Sometimes some of the scientific journals are difficult to get. I had trouble with a copy of *Scientific American* of three years back once. (*Technical journalist*)

In general, then, library members are satisfied with the books available and with the reference service. The small minority who use the gramophone record service find that it has limitations. There are obviously gaps in the libraries' ability to cater for specialist or specialised requirements and these gaps are bound on the whole to be experienced more in branch libraries than in main or central ones.

**Cataloguing**

There are, as experienced library users know as well as librarians, a number of ways in which books, records and other materials may or may not be 'available'. A library may not stock a particular title; it may stock it in several copies, all of which have been borrowed already or reserved by other members; it may stock a book but not display it on the open shelves, which tends to happen not only to the esoteric and the erotic but also to reference books and to standard works for which there is little current demand. If a member of a library does not consult a member of the staff, but simply examines the shelves in their morning order or their Saturday afternoon chaos, he does not know precisely whether and in what sense a book is available at all. He is, however, in a strong position to know these things – almost as strong as the library personnel – if he has a keen eye and can use the catalogue.

About a quarter of all the members interviewed were not in this desirable position, and the total so handicapped may be even higher because interviewers met people who said that they found the cataloguing system satisfactory and then revealed in conversation that they did not know what it was. However, 12 per cent of the members said they were dissatisfied with it – for them its use was limited; and over 13 per cent of them admitted they did not know enough about it to express an opinion – for them it was a mystery. Thus a company director complained, 'It's so profound, it's beyond me', an archaeologist called it 'a problem', and a private secretary confessed, 'I find it very confusing – I don't find time for the index system'. Classification schemes and catalogue systems differ, as a constructional engineer had discovered, 'I've used a better one in another library – one I was able to get the hang of without asking the staff'. Sometimes people said that there was no catalogue at all for the one part of the stock in which they were interested – 'The fiction books are not really catalogued – that's mostly what I go for'.

**Borrowing and returning machinery**

Another potential source of dissatisfaction with the library service lies in the machinery for returning, renewing and reserving books, including the inter-library loan scheme, but only eight respondents were in any way dissatisfied with the system of returning books; the same number were dissatisfied with the renewal system, and most respondents were content to give monosyllabic answers about them. A few commented on the length of time for which books could be kept (which was regarded as reasonable by most):

A month is long enough to read a book. (*Housewife*)

The period is long enough. I never have any trouble. (*Business woman*)

Some thought the time was too short, including a solicitor's clerk, who said, 'I would like to be able to borrow a book for more than a fortnight and also take out more than three at a time'. (Regulations about the number of books that can be borrowed and the length of time for which they can be borrowed differ between libraries).

To test whether members knew that they could reserve books, and to make sure that their opinions were based on experience, they were first asked simply, 'Can you reserve books in your library?' If they said 'yes', the supplementary was put: 'Have you ever tried to reserve a book?' If they said 'yes' again, they were asked whether the system worked well or not. Over 80 per cent of the members said they could reserve books in their library. Two respondents said they could not and the rest did not know. That some 20 per cent of the library members should be unaware of this facility may be a cause of some astonishment to some readers of this report. It is surely a reminder to librarians not to assume that their patrons know all they need. Of those who did know about the reservation facilities, about three-quarters had reserved books, and the majority found the facilities satisfactory. Twelve people had some criticism to make and were not quite so complimentary. These comments were typical:

I've never had to wait too long. (*Telephone engineer*)

Generally have to wait one week. (*Trainee quantity surveyor*)

If a book is in demand they let you know that it is. I've always had the book I've asked for in time. (*Tailor*)

Very successful. Last time I reserved a book it took three days – that's not so bad. (*Electrical engineer*)

You get the book in the end but you often have to wait – they might have more copies of books much in demand and the same for records – you may have to wait more than a month. (*Electrical engineer*)

I have reserved a couple of books. I waited about a month each time. I think to wait a month for a book, if it's a good library, is too long. (*Receptionist*)

Some respondents thought it was an unsatisfactory procedure partly because of the fee:

You can on payment of sixpence but I had to wait a long time. (*Secretary*)

Too expensive and it means waiting too long. (*Senior Government official*)

Even prompt service sometimes arouses suspicion:

My only complaint is that you have to pay sixpence just for them to get it from downstairs. (*Teacher*)

And there were others who were not sure that the system is operated fairly:

I've got doubts about the strictness of the priority lists. (*Secretary*)

I am convinced that there is a reserved stock that is kept underground. I don't think they keep all their books on display. You fill in a card and pay sixpence and it comes the very next day. (*Housewife, former teacher*)

A similar procedure was used to test reactions to the inter-library loans scheme, starting with the question: 'Can your library borrow books from other libraries?' Only just over half of the members knew that it could, and all but four of the others said they did not know. The four were sure that no such reciprocal arrangement existed. Just under half of those who knew the service existed had used it and all but five found it satisfactory. Some of the library members interviewed heard of the system for the first time during the course of the interview, like the typist who said, 'I didn't know that was possible – how interesting'.

**Regulations**

Nearly everyone interviewed felt you could not have a service of this kind without some rules and regulations. Indeed, only two per cent thought the regulations unreasonable. But 'regulations' was narrowly construed – the time allowed for reading books and the fines imposed were the only two aspects that members seemed to be concerned with. Those (one per cent) who thought the regulations were acceptable only (as distinct from 'reasonable' or 'unreasonable') were all concerned with the length of the loan period:

If you keep them after a week, you pay and keep on paying. (*Waiter – used the library once a month*)

I should think the lending time should be three weeks. (*Archaeologist*)

Respondents were also asked a separate question about fines. Far from attracting criticism fining was looked upon with approval by about half the members. A third were non-commital on the subject and six per cent objected to the application of fines in particular cases. Only four people objected on principle:

I think they're reasonable. I've got four tickets and if I take four books out and can't read them I should be fined. (*Packer and checker*)

Not too bad. Only sixpence a week if you're overdue. (*Labourer*)

Some feel that fines are light (they vary from borough to borough):

I think it's a good idea – it's a nasty thing if people hang on to a book while you're waiting – probably not enough is charged. (*Housewife*)

Fines are regarded as a deterrent to those who would otherwise keep books too long or damage them (they sometimes serve, as the last chapter showed, to deter people right out of membership):

I've never been fined yet. The fine is ten shillings at Westminster.* It's a good deterrent for anybody who does not return books. (*Civil Servant*)

There must be a token fine or people would be careless and waste the books and make them dirty. (*School cook*)

Fines are not stiff enough at times, when they find books with dreadful words written in. Sometimes they get books badly handled, papers torn out and everything. I think they should be stiffer. A person that borrows a book should give it back in the same condition as he got it in. I don't have to pay fines – the time's enough. (*Housewife*)

Fines for multilation were supported by a shop assistant:

There is nothing worse than a torn book. One book I remember I got to the last page and it wasn't there! It spoiled the whole book for me!

A few did object to fines:

They're a bit unreasonable as regards records. The school mislaid some records and the librarian wanted me to pay on the dot. (*Teacher*)

Fines are a bugbear to me. I don't think they should charge a penny a day after a fortnight. It's hard on people who are slow readers. I think it would be better if it was a fixed amount weekly; say, threepence. (*Widow*)

* This is the maximum fine for losing one's membership token, not a fine for exceeding the loan period which is one penny per day.

Some objected not for themselves but for others:

> I don't think Old Age Pensioners should be charged for a period to cover illness. Some can't get someone to go for them when they are ill. (*Housewife*)

**Impression of staff**

After the library's stock and the ease with which it is made available, the library staff are likely to affect satisfaction or dissatisfaction with the service more than any other aspect of provision. Even if there are difficulties in obtaining books the reader may be more prepared to accept delays when the librarians are helpful and interested. The numbers and kind of staff required are constant preoccupations of the profession and are matters of some complexity. Members were, however, asked a simple straightforward question: 'What is your general impression of the staff?' They were asked to rate them very good, good, adequate, fair or poor. Half thought the staff were 'very good'; only seven out of 160 members were prepared to classify them as 'fair' or 'poor'. The most commendatory respondents made comments like these:

> Very, very courteous. (*Lift erector*)
>
> Very helpful, sociable, friendly. (*Fitter and turner*)
>
> Never had any trouble, I don't expect much more; they do put themselves out. (*Despatch manager*)
>
> Very helpful. Very polite. Never had one who is indifferent to your requirements. Never one who is rude or ill-bred. (*Companion help*)
>
> They go out of their way to help you. (*Shorthand typist*)

A further third of the members thought that staffs were 'good'. This assessment was sometimes qualified by such remarks as the chartered accountant's 'when they weren't busy'.

Some people managed to use their library without coming into contact with the staff:

> Don't have much to do with them. (*Housewife*)
>
> Good, but I haven't spoken to them. I only get the books stamped. (*Plastics chemist*)
>
> Photocharging – so I don't have much to do with them. (*Chemist*)

Just under one in eight of the members felt the staff were 'adequate':

> No complaints. (*Bank messenger*)
>
> Some are good – on the whole adequate. (*Designer in advertising*)

A few blamed inadequacies on part-time staffing:

> Today she was very helpful, but often they are not because they take on part-time staff. (*Schoolgirl*)

Then, lastly, there were those few who thought the staff on the whole 'fair' or 'poor':

Some librarians are not very helpful. It would be better if they were all helpful. (*Housewife, former kindergarten teacher*)

They are slow – the assistants, that is. (*Book-keeper and cashier*)

They don't look up authors or books for you and are so busy I don't like to ask. I don't know how to look up the index and the staff are too busy to show me. Also I didn't like to say I didn't know how to use an index like that one. (*Transport supervisor*)

Depends on the chap or girl. You do get the highbrow sort of person. Haven't got too much time for you. But I wouldn't say too much against them. (*Clerical assistant*)

On the whole, then, library staffs were strongly praised, and this indicates a situation that is in many ways desirable and satisfactory. But the members' evaluation needs itself to be evaluated, by being compared with their apparent expectations. It will be remembered that the non-members also had a favourable impression of the staff, but that this was associated with a rather narrow view of their functions. It now appears that the members' view is almost as narrow. 'The staff are very good' serves often to mean not much more than 'The staff are well-mannered'. It was rare indeed for anyone to speak, as the transport supervisor just quoted did, about the specific technical assistance that might be received. And the comments of this Civil Service clerical officer were unique: 'I don't really know these days what's required of a librarian. I always thought they'd perhaps know the authors of books you wanted. I usually look round and find my own. They are not particularly enthusiastic. They seem to change a lot. They don't seem as interested as they ought to be.'

**Satisfaction with library buildings**

Poor libraries manned by unhelpful staffs could not be redeemed by beautiful buildings, but as the piles inherited from Carnegie and Tate are often viewed as barriers between the library and its potential readership, members were asked about four physical attributes of libraries: the outside appearance (attractive, off-putting, or neither?); the appearance and layout inside; the lighting and the furniture. The following table (Table 34) shows how the members regarded these four aspects.

As might be expected, the outside appearance of libraries was rated least favourably. In the seven boroughs there are some new buildings which are much admired and were remarked on in the interviews, but there are also buildings which are a legacy of the institutional provision for the Victorian poor; however, there seems no reason to assume that the

Table 34 Members' satisfaction with the buildings

| | Well satisfied (per cent) | Fairly satisfied (per cent) | Not satisfied (per cent) |
|---|---|---|---|
| Outside appearance | 56 | 21 | 23 |
| Inside layout | 76 | 16 | 8 |
| Furniture | 63 | 30 | 7 |
| Lighting | 57 | 39 | 4 |

external appearance of the library has any untoward effect on those who are already members. Most people would probably agree with the company secretary who said, 'It doesn't matter to me really'. However, when asked about external appearance, several members were moved to praise not only the new buildings but the old as well:

It's just been opened, very modern and up to date. (*Radio dealer*)

It was part of the old Lewisham as I knew it. I like the old very much. (*Companion housekeeper*)

For some their library building even exerts a fascination:

Attractive – especially in the evening when it's lit up. (*Foreman warehouseman*)

There was a sense that a library ought to be distinctive in some way:

It was jolly up there in the other one on Dorset Estate [in an adjacent borough]. This one at Sidney Street is only a very small place – there is nothing generous about it. It's just like an ordinary little brick building. The Dorset one was circular and had windows all the way round. It was more modern. (*Dressmaker*)

It's not one of the nicer ones I have seen. It's not unpleasant. Some libraries make one think they look nice but not this one – perhaps because it's on a corner. (*Clerk in a chainstore*)

One respondent mentioned that it was not clear from the outside of his nearest one what the building's function was. There was nothing to say it was a library.

There were many others who were less restrained in their comments. The appearance of the library they used provoked them to a range of pejoratives:

Like a morgue or an old church. (*Transport supervisor*)

Dreadful. (*Architect*)

Rather old and a bit off-putting. (*Apprentice*)

Grimy, depressing. (*Superintendent in an electric service company*)

Institutional, as they mostly are. (*Company director*)

It looks like a cross between a church and a prison. (*Construction engineer*)

*Layout and lighting*

Although there was little outright dissatisfaction with lighting, there was a large section of these members who only rated it 'adequate'. (Hampstead, Finsbury and Chelsea came in for rather more than their share of criticism.) Although lighting is not the kind of subject that provokes much detailed comment from laymen, there were remarks that implied its functional and psychological importance:

> Lighting is good even without lights on. They're nice big windows. Very good upstairs too. (*Housewife*)
>
> Could read anything, and there are lamps on the tables. (*Secretary*)
>
> Dismal entrance hall, too dark to read the nice new notices they put up. (*Transport supervisor*)

The question about the interior coupled 'appearance' and 'layout', but there were very few criticisms about either. For instance, in Stepney only one respondent was critical. In all boroughs there was a high degree of satisfaction:

> Well labelled and well laid out. (*Packer and checker*)
>
> Beautiful, very well done, a very good library, good clean, best I've ever been in. (*Constructional engineer*)
>
> Very good. They've gone to town just lately. (*Draughtsman*)

Adverse criticism was often directed at layout, rather than general appearance:

> Outdated as last week's breakfast. (*Superintendent, electrical company*)
>
> Pleasant appearance but very confusing arrangement. The history section is comprehensive but could be indexed more usefully. Plays, fiction, etc., are confusing to locate. (*Drama student*)
>
> The numbers don't run in sequence so you have to go from one end to the other. (*Trainee quantity surveyor*)
>
> Seems a bit of a jumble. Racks at angles and not in straight lines. (*Apprentice*)
>
> Not keen on the arrangement of books but it's absolutely spotless. (*Warehouse foreman*)
>
> A mess – not meant to be a library. Needs renovating. (*Student*)

The furniture came in for slightly more criticism than the general inside appearance of the library. Perhaps many were like the respondent who said, 'I don't think there is any!', but some had taken sufficient notice of what was provided to be able to comment on it:

> Couches all round the outside of the main room. Very comfortable. No room for central chairs and tables. I suppose it might be a good idea to have these for Old Age Pensioners. (*Housewife*)

Round tables, wooden chairs with padded seats are quite comfortable. (*Packer and checker*)

Should be more chairs. (*Labourer on building site*)

They've got a problem there. A number of unemployed use it to keep warm I expect. (*Civil Servant*)

A bit old – heavy wooden tables. (*Apprentice*)

Usual hard seats. (*Draughtsman*)

I don't think it would be very comfortable if you were sitting there a long time. (*Tally clerk*)

Rather austere, seats could be more comfortable. (*Student*)

Once again, judgment seemed sometimes to be conditioned by habitual expectations. As one respondent put it, 'When I go to the library I don't expect to find a lounge'. Somehow the idea of real comfort is barely compatible with the idea of a library. In any case it is the books which count most:

Adequate – within costs I'd rather have a good service than good furniture. (*Depot inspector*)

And, by and large, it is clear that the majority of these members think that they are getting a good service. In order to 'place' this judgment in some kind of perspective, the library members were asked what they thought of some other public services – local, regional and national. The question was put: 'How well do you think these other public services are doing their job on the whole?' and a choice of answers was offered – 'Excellent/good/adequate or fair/poor'. The other public services asked about were refuse collection, the electricity board, income tax and London Transport. Having accustomed respondents to the five categories, interviewers then added 'and the Public Libraries?'

The following table (Table 35) shows the distribution of the answers:

Table 35 Members' satisfaction with other public services

| | Excellent/good | | Adequate | | Fair/poor | | Totals | |
|---|---|---|---|---|---|---|---|---|
| | Number | Per cent | Number | Per cent | Number | Per cent | Number* | Per cent |
| Refuse collection | 83 | 57 | 40 | 26 | 23 | 17 | 146 | 100 |
| Electricity Board | 78 | 52 | 51 | 34 | 20 | 14 | 149 | 100 |
| Income tax | 45 | 36 | 44 | 36 | 36 | 28 | 125 | 100 |
| London Transport | 32 | 22 | 42 | 29 | 73 | 49 | 147 | 100 |
| Public libraries | 153 | 97 | 4 | 3 | 1 | † | 158 | 100 |

* Difference between totals and the sample total of 160 shows the number who were unable to reply to the question.

† Less than one per cent.

There seems to be little doubt about it: if he belongs to one, the Londoner likes his library.

# Chapter 9

# Commentary: libraries and the community

It is not proposed in this commentary to judge the library services in the seven boroughs, still less to prescribe improvements in them. Inevitably much that is said will apply to them, either by suggesting reforms that might be considered there and elsewhere, or by commending practices which they have already adopted. But this chapter has a broader purpose: to examine some of the issues facing the public library service in the light of what the survey has discovered about the public.

## Goodwill and progress

It might be tempting, in the first place, to draw comfort from the previous chapter's conclusion: here, apparently, is a public service held in exceptionally high regard by its patrons. It may be that these Londoners are fortunate because the library services to which most of them belonged are among the best in the country, but even so their specific and general expressions of satisfaction seem to have little in common with the verdicts of critics within and without the public library world. The critic from the profession might use D. E. Gerard's tone:

> Decades of devitalizing talk about the neutral role of the local government officer have produced a public service which is an efficient nullity, and that includes us in the public libraries, to our shame. (*The Library Association Record*, August 1963.)

The lay critic, on the other hand, might endorse the words of Sir Alan Herbert, dissenting even from Gerard's assumption of efficiency:

> The public libraries . . . are inefficient, or at least deficient . . . a public institution created by Parliament is failing to satisfy its customers . . . the supply of books to the readers is far from satisfactory. (*Libraries: Free-for-All?*, pp. 30–38.)

ASLIB,* in a statement sent to the Ministry of Education, noted with a touch of irony that the Roberts Committee Report and the two Working Party reports assume 'that the purpose of the whole library system is to satisfy readers', but the statement went on to observe that 'Little attempt seems to have been made to find out how far readers are in fact satisfied

* Association of Special Libraries and Information Bureaux.

at present'. Other references suggest that ASLIB probably had in mind consumer research so extensive that the survey reported here might only serve as a useful prologue to it, but it is perhaps simultaneously disconcerting and gratifying to find that this attempt to find out 'how far' readers were satisfied showed them reasonably well satisfied.*

An optimist might see this discovery as the creditable conclusion to a progressive history: in 1924 there were two-and-a-half million borrowers from public libraries, and the libraries claimed 76 million issues. Today (1964) there are over 13 million borrowers and issues are running at something like 440 million a year. Expenditure on books has gone up even in the last few years from just under £4 million a year when the Roberts Committee was sitting to £6 million a year in 1962–63, not all of the rise being caused by higher prices. The unevenness of provision throughout the country has been thoroughly documented as never before by the three official reports: all political parties agree in principle on legislation to empower the Department of Education and Science to insist on minimum standards of efficiency from library authorities. It could be argued that what is mainly needed is that more authorities should spend at least as liberally on books and staff as do the libraries in the seven boroughs where this survey was conducted. In the same optimistic mood it is possible to contemplate the future, along with the Working Party report on Standards:

> As for the years to come, we have no doubt that progressively higher standards will be set as the importance of the public library service to the life of the nation comes to be increasingly recognised.†

It is only fair to recognise that this account of progress is true as far as it goes. Even to raise standards throughout the country to a level comparable to that achieved by these seven boroughs (as measured by the kind of criteria by which the Department of Education and Science will in future have to assess an authority's fitness to supply a library service) would indeed represent substantial progress in many areas.

But when the emphasis turns from the facts of provision to the people for whom the provision is made, as in this report, the outcome is chastening. The popular prestige of public libraries is immense; hardly a word will anyone say against them. And yet most people do not belong to them; specific criticisms of them are made by non-members, former members and members (not merely of those in the seven boroughs, for many of the comments made were intended much more generally) of such a kind and on such a scale as to throw serious doubt on their adequacy; and even the praise which the libraries evoke partly reflects the meagreness of public

* *ASLIB Proceedings*, **15**, 8, August 1963.

† *Standards of Public Library Service in England and Wales*, p. 4.

expectations: a library is just a place where you change your books, and a librarian is like the girl at the supermarket checkout. In short, the regard in which public libraries are held should be taken by the profession and the authorities as a precious asset, as goodwill with which to make more progress possible, rather than a sign that enough has been achieved.

**The potential public**

The Victorian poor, for whose redemption the libraries were created, are no longer with us; but the need for public libraries will rapidly become much greater than it is today, as society becomes more literate. There is more to this than the continuous increase in the number of students in the population, the aspect most often stressed. As all aspects of life are more influenced by technical change and less by tradition, the more important will everyone find literacy throughout life to be. Already, for instance, the felt inadequacies of much industrial training are matched by the need for literacy in the home; it is the epoch of complicated labelling instructions, cookery books and child care from Dr Spock.* It will soon become even less feasible than it is today for anyone to own or find room for all the books and other aids that will be needed for an efficient life, let alone a full one. Not enough libraries seem to be preparing and practising for the pressure to come.

The present demands being made on public libraries are relatively light, because Britain is only a partly literate country. Large numbers of people are disfranchised or discouraged from making use of what libraries have to offer by their inability to read – 'I get halfway through the *Mirror* and that's my lot'. It is not inevitable that so many people should be backward readers, but it is a fact that they are and it is not one for which the public libraries are responsible.

Nor are librarians mainly responsible for the men and women who have left school without having been introduced to the amenities of public libraries. Many members owe their membership in part to the encouragement they received at school; it is reasonable to assume that more encouragement, in a variety of forms – a contagious delight in books, attractive school libraries, and growing familiarity with modern techniques of storing information – would lead to more members (remembering, as always, that this is a short way of saying that more people, knowing what choices were open to them, would have the desire and the confidence to make this one).

This is the background against which the achievement of the libraries in making contact with the public has to be judged. The inadequacies of

* Dr B. Spock's *Baby and Child Care* is said to have sold over 15 million copies; people used to learn how to bring up babies from their mothers.

many people's education make libraries, or, at any rate, their chief stock-in-trade, nearly as irrelevant to them as they patently are to most children under four and to the very ill. The library's potential public is limited by the stimulus or the damage that it has received from other aspects of social life.

About a quarter of the 500 people interviewed were just not particularly interested in reading; moreover, the replies of the former members show how easy it is to be altogether dislodged – by leaving school, by getting married, by having a baby – from the habit of library use.* These facts are needed to give some reality not only to professional talk in the abstract about standards but also to observations about the taste of people who do use public libraries:

> We are spending approximately £20 million a year on 440 million borrowed books. No less than 60 per cent of these are romances, adventure stories, Westerns, detective stories and humour. . . . I ask the House seriously to consider what principle requires the State-educated and prosperous wage-earner to obtain free from his public library (such) books . . . at the expense of the elderly widow's rates. . . . (T. L. Iremonger, MP, in the Commons, 5 February 1964.)

Leaving aside the polemical implications of Mr Iremonger's speech on the Public Libraries and Museums Bill (and the wildness of his figures), it should be remembered – and it is no doubt genuinely difficult for people with talent and authority to do this – that to go regularly to a public library to borrow light fiction is to exercise more initiative and to show more cultural resourcefulness than most people in the population do.

Although the relevance of a public library to someone's needs may depend more in the first instance on his home, neighbourhood and school than on the library only, that is no reason for libraries to wait passively for those with the previously developed competence to make use of them; it is certainly not a reason for tolerating features – ugly buildings pervaded by an official atmosphere, inappropriate stocks obscurely displayed – which actively discourage people, through unfortunate experience or disquieting reputation, from ever joining or from staying in membership. There are people who mistakenly believe they have no use for books as well as those who know that books are beyond them; there are people who may not like reading, but who could enjoy a book of Van Gogh or Ben Shahn reproductions, or gramophone records of *The Mikado*, *West Side Story* or the King's College Chapel ceremony of carols.

* The extent to which library membership is left behind with school was shown in the Crowther report: 'Over half the modern schoolboys and girls interviewed for us . . . had at one time belonged to a public library; only 16 per cent still belonged two years after leaving school.' *Fifteen to Eighteen*: para. 171, p. 112.

In this sense, those librarians who believe some sociological understanding of the people in their areas to be an essential complement to their professional skills, are surely those likely to advance the service to new levels of public relevance and successful provision.*

## A heterogeneous public

> I used to read serials in *Woman* and then I found you could get the same serial published in book form. (*Part-time dressmaker*)
>
> My mates at school got books out on fishing. I saw their books and joined the same library. (*Waiter*)
>
> I work in reproduction antiques, and there were things I didn't know, so I went there to use their technical books. (*Mill foreman*)
>
> I found I needed so many books as a student which I could not afford to buy, so I joined the public library. (*Television engineer*)

It is a mistake to think of public library users as a particular class of people, a rather narrow strand from the middle class, for instance. It is true that library members are more likely to be drawn from members of the public with some education after the age of 15 than from those who left school at the statutory minimum, more likely to be ex-grammar school pupils than ex-secondary modern and elementary school, and more likely to be middle class than working class. But this is not to say much more than that libraries do not at present attract members from different sections of the community in proportion to their numbers in the population. The membership of any particular library, depending on the skill and imagination with which it is run, and on the enthusiasm with which it is backed by the community (especially the schools), may be composed of as varied a mixture of men and women as reside or work in the neighbourhood.

There is some danger that too much concern with 'standards' in a void – how many volumes and which titles should every self-respecting library system hold? – and too little concern with the people for whom the service is intended, could make libraries more 'efficient' than they are at present, but not much more 'effective', that is, not bringing more benefits to more people. In this respect, apart from anomalies caused in practice by different loan periods and other factors, the number of issues per head is a more important criterion than, for instance, expenditure per head or numbers of volumes added to stock annually, simply because it is a criterion which expresses the *service relationship* between library and user. The kind of

* Dr G. Chandler, Liverpool City librarian, described a specialised use of sociological data in the Liverpool central libraries at the Library Association's Public Libraries Conference, 1963. (*Proceedings of the Public Libraries Conference*, The Library Association, 1963.)

stock of books and other materials which a library system holds should be related to the people living or working in its catchment areas, and the deployment of stock through its branches and other service points must reflect as sensitively as possible the tastes and needs of the people living round them.

Unless it is immediately qualified, many librarians will reject this statement as retrogressive, fearing that, if taken seriously, it would mean their ceasing to be a profession and turning into some kind of civic restaurateur, opportunistically setting up branches in one place filled with learned texts for 'Dip. Tech.' students and in another creating branches in which Hank Janson and romantic novels were the most demanding alternatives to the pop record bar.

This is a familiar and quite unnecessary dilemma: on the horns of it, intellectuals with democratic convictions affect ignorance and philistinism. The alternative to a bibliographically impeccable library which hardly anyone uses is not one packed to the ceiling with rabid collectors of the lurid and the trivial. The community has set up schools of librarianship to train people to know more than the rest of us about books, so that they can decide or advise what should be bought on our behalf. (This might properly involve knowing what romantic novels, Westerns and detective stories are the best of their kind. A reader is more likely to develop insight into human character from reading Siménon than from reading either a hack police novel or a novel with a stronger claim to being literature which was unfortunately beyond his understanding.)

Naturally there is a tension between the professional belief that a worthwhile library includes certain books and materials and not others, and the professional desire to serve the public on terms of its own commissioning. But it is better (and more democratic) to endure this tension than to cater solely for élite sections of the population (which is what Berelson recommends), or to talk generally about the greatly increased numbers of people whose scientific and technological training will lead to increased demands on public libraries – without wondering how true that would be from place to place (which is what could happen if library committees were too uncritical of contemporary speechmakers); it is certainly better than what seems to happen in too many libraries at present.*

Public libraries too often seem to consist of 'ideal' collections, modified

* 'The adult library *clientèle* is relatively small . . . universality of . . . service is practically impossible. . . . It may be, therefore, that the librarian should explicitly redefine his goal from attempting to serve the total community to providing the minority of "serious" users . . . with the tools which they need.' (*The Library's Public*, B. Berelson, New York, Columbia University Press, 1949, pp. 129 e.s.)

at both ends: at one end by a crippling lack of money to implement the ideal, at the other end by readers' requests for specific works which are bought when they are not borrowed from elsewhere. But a public library's stock (as distinct from a university library's on the one hand, or a commercial library's on the other) ought not to be a scholar's imperfect collection bent into viable shape or forced into embarrassed compromises by consumer demand: given the population scale on which library authorities will increasingly operate, the stock ought to be a purposively contrived blend of major works and ephemeral materials, reaching appropriate standards according to the class of material, and likely to be put to optimum use by all significant majority and minority segments of the population.

The 'ideal' character of collections can be achieved only by public and other libraries effectively co-operating together, for only in this way can they be sure of being able to respond to any demand, however specialised.

Lastly, as the comments about layout and catalogues showed, users and potential users differ not only in their tastes and purposes: they also differ in the extent to which they know what they want and in their ability to find or ask for what they want in a library. Successful libraries can, of course, be run for readily identified sections of the public, but libraries which wish to be truly *public* libraries should reflect the heterogeneity of that public, at the authority level and down to the branch level. This would enable them to give better service to those who belong; less dispensable service for people who can lapse so casually; and less awesome service for those who have hitherto thought that libraries were only for other people.

This statement about public libraries and the public has assumed that it is right to relate the service, in principle and in practice, to all three of these sections of the public. The paragraphs that follow are brief application of the thesis to a range of specific issues raised by the survey.

## Practical issues

(i) *Publicity*

No doubt a good library is its own best advertisement. But the usefulness of members in recommending the services of a good library to their friends and neighbours is thrown in doubt by the discovery that many members have only a limited knowledge of what their library does. So considerable was the lack of awareness in the seven surveyed boroughs, that libraries surely need to improve their publicity in two directions – outwards to the general public, and internally to present members. Many librarians have felt for some time that their services ought to be better publicised, and now, perhaps, it becomes a little clearer how this generalised desire might be translated into a programme.

There are, of course, other librarians who do not approve of publicity, because to them it conveys the unprofessional atmosphere of 'advertising', 'market research' and other equally suspect activities. The object of publicity is not, however, to turn librarians into salesmen; it is to increase the use made of the resource materials of which librarians are the professional custodians; it is to tell more people of utilities available to them, because directly or indirectly they already pay for them; it is to educate the community in what a public library is and does.

The advice of the youth worker Stanley Rowe is evidently applicable beyond the age range which is his speciality:

> The librarian needs to sell his books like the good cinema manager sells his films. He has got to get them in the news and the greater use of the local newspaper would catch some young people's eye.*

New acquisitions and special events would often make good copy; the stories that librarians relate in their (limited circulation) annual reports about the use that people make of their services show that there are many humanly interesting ways in which they could spread the understanding that they are not learned warehousemen, but people whose work could enliven, enlighten and refresh the lives of men and women of all kinds. Local publicity could usefully be reinforced from time to time by national campaigns; 12–18 April 1964 was National Library Week in the United States and was widely publicised by the mass media; *Esquire* magazine, for example, told its readers about it in captions every few pages in the April 1964 issue and carried an article commending librarianship as a profession. This device is to be attempted in Britain; it needs to be backed by a continuing and many-sided campaign.

The seven boroughs do in fact spend money on publicity – people interviewed in Finsbury, for instance, had heard of the new St Luke's branch because of the well-designed handbills that went through their doors; Stepney has published annotated booklists about special interests – there is one on fishing, for example; Lewisham has issued a brochure of cartoons illustrating reasons why readers might want to use its services ('Why not bring that knotty problem to the Reference Library? – or if your children belong to the library you may have sufficient peace at home to solve it there'). But many people remain oblivious, despite these efforts. They do not know that Braille books may be borrowed through London libraries, or that a variety of tastes are catered for by gramophone record collections; they do not even know that public libraries lend light fiction. L. J. Sharpe

*Proceedings* of the Annual Conference, The Library Association, 1962.

found (in *The Metropolis Votes*) that many people do not know who runs the public library service; much more serious, from the librarian's point of view, is their not knowing what it can offer them.*

(ii) *The right books*

There is probably no worse criticism to be made of a public library than that the books a reader wants are not available from it. Nearly a fifth of the non-members feared this would be so; nearly a quarter of the former members had lapsed because they had found it was so; and in all a third of the members confirmed it, to a greater or lesser degree. Many readers were not too disturbed by this, and others reserved their criticism for branch libraries. But the Working Party on Standards rightly observed that the unit which has to be tested for efficiency is precisely this basic unit: the branch. Criticism on this scale of the availability of books, especially as it was partly prompted by libraries in metropolitan London, is evidence not consistent with a satisfactory service.

Obviously no branch library can carry all the books and materials that people might need at the moment when they ask for them. Popular works may not be on the shelves, though many copies are bought; other books may have to be transferred from the central library or from another branch; yet others would have to be borrowed from another London library. An official brochure explains the scheme already referred to in Chapter 2 through which the London libraries 'collect every book published in this country no matter how specialised', each library holds part of the complete collection, and the stock is available to all Londoners. The efficiency of the service depends then on the size of local stocks and the speed with which items not stocked locally can be moved. The shorthand typist quoted (p. 75) had found that 'heavier reading' was not so well catered for – 'one book took nearly three months to get'.

To gain first-hand experience of this rather than to establish anything that could be called research findings, RICA asked some registered users in the seven boroughs to reserve books that were not too esoteric and which they genuinely wanted – some were listed in the catalogue but were not on the shelves, and others were not in the catalogue. This is what happened to the reservations of books in the catalogue but already out on loan: The Opies' *The Lore and Language of Schoolchildren* (notification received in eleven days), Foot's biography of Aneurin Bevan (eight weeks), J. K. Stanford's *Ladies in the Sun* (five weeks), and Rose Macaulay's *Letters to a Friend* (three days, including a Sunday). The books borrowed

* *The Metropolis Votes*, L. J. Sharpe, Greater London Papers no. 8, London School of Economics, 1962.

from other libraries were these: Jennings' *Societies in the Making* (twelve days), E. Evans-Pritchard's *Nuer Religion* (two months, seven days), *Introduction to Statistical Method* by B. C. Brookes and W. F. L. Dick (just over two months), selected or collected plays of Brecht in original (school edition of one play received ten weeks later).

All the people who recorded their experiences complimented the staff on their helpfulness, which usually included a fairly accurate prediction of the delay. Sometimes a book was swiftly located, but surely some of the delays experienced vitiate the usefulness of the service? 'Every public library', according to the report on Standards, 'should be not only a storehouse in itself but a gateway to the full resources of the region and of the country' (p. 7). Is eleven weeks a reasonable time to wait in the porch? How many consumers would find their ardour unquenched and their interest as sharp after such a wait?

There is some doubt, then, about the satisfactoriness even of the metropolitan libraries' scheme in this respect. The danger is a real one: libraries that are inadequately stocked and linked by cumbersome inter-lending schemes are likely to be libraries that cater best for casual readers, rather than for purposive ones, and to do best of all for the reader who does not mind much what he reads, 'as long as it's a good book'. Such readers have every right to be looked after; indeed they are most readers at some times, but they hardly encourage a library to develop good muscle tone. They were probably the people that D. E. Gerard had in mind when he wrote (again in his 'efficient nullity' letter): 'the most frightening and sobering result of this . . . is simply that we have got the readers we deserved, as toneless and dull as ourselves'. When it comes to abusing the customers, anger has perhaps been unleashed rather indiscriminately – and yet there is a truth there: going to a library is for many people most of the time and for some people occasionally more like going to a jumble sale for bargains than going to the town's best store to make a calculated and deliberate purchase.

(iii) *Gramophone records and other materials*

Gramophone record collections have publicity value and help to undermine out-dated conceptions of what public libraries are like. Many of the people interviewed did not know that there were record collections, and some of them were under the impression (quite unjustified in most of these boroughs) that they could only borrow classical music. But record libraries are no novelty – some of them in London started in the late 1940s. A survey carried out in 1961 found that 13 London libraries provided light music, eight jazz, ten folk music, 13 speech, 12 complete plays and 11 language records, but this same survey deplored the 'different standard applied to gramophone record provision compared to book provision'.* It is not so surprising, therefore, that comments about it were unenthusiastic – 'You have to take your pick from what's left, not what you want'. The Working Party had only a one-sentence recommendation to make: 'We consider that the provision for loan of non-book material, such as gramophone records, art reproductions, films and other visual aids is an increasingly important part of the public library service' (p. 26). It neither inspires nor does it make clear what standards should be aimed at, but at least it has led to a usefully comprehensive reference in the Public Libraries and Museum Bill.†

(iv) *Reference*

In the House of Commons' debate (5 February 1964) on the Public Libraries and Museums Bill, the Member for Caernarvon, Mr Goronwy Roberts, criticised 'the out-of-date, inadequate, disappointing condition of the reference sections. . . . The general picture we have is of people asking for the loan of recent works of fiction but . . . I have found that a surprising number of people use the reference sections'. London is the centre for so many special libraries that the metropolitan borough libraries can concentrate more on services for general readers, who seem to benefit particularly from the standard of reference sections. These prompted little criticism.

The principal issue here is probably one with which the survey did not deal: for whom are reference rooms chiefly provided? At present many public libraries are relieving the pressure on technical college and other libraries, but in the absence of a national plan to co-ordinate library resources. The Department of Education is better placed to take the appropriate initiative than its predecessors.

(v) *Finding the books; being helped by the staff*

(1) Look in the card catalogue under author, subject or title. You will find on each card the classification number by which the book is shelved; cards for novels bear the letter 'F'.

* *The London Librarian*, **8**, 1, January 1962. (See also *Gramophone Record Libraries*, ed. H. F. J. Currall, Crosby Lockwood, 1963.)

† 'In fulfilling its duty . . . a library authority shall in particular have regard to the desirability . . . of securing, by the keeping of adequate stocks, by arrangements with other library authorities, and by any other appropriate means, that facilities are available for the borrowing of, or reference to, books and other printed matter, and pictures, gramophone records, films and other materials, sufficient in number, range and quality to meet the general requirements and any special requirements both of adults and children.' (Bill 67/1964, para. 7.)

> (2) Look on the shelves for the section with that number. For novels look in the fiction section under the name of the author. The staff are always ready to help. The card catalogue contains entries for all books whether they are on the shelves or on loan.

Thus part of a leaflet issued by Hampstead Public Libraries.

> There's such a lot of books up there. You walk round them quite a bit. You don't really know what books they've got, unless it's one you really want and than you ask them if they've got it.

Thus, the spontaneous comment of a library user (others similar were quoted on p. 78). Several of the people interviewed, though disconcerted by the catalogue, found the staff helpful either in explaining it or in locating books without its assistance. The staff, after all, are less distressed by features of the Dewey classification system which may make little sense to ordinary library users.

The technical problems involved in lucid cataloguing, fruitful cross-referencing, and shelf guiding are familiar to librarians. This makes it surprising that there is not more positive sympathy shown for the reader who may be quickly overwhelmed by the sheer quantity of books that surround him. Hence, probably, the popularity of that little pre-selected library within a library – the shelves for returned books: not too many of them, all commended because all recently borrowed, not at all threatening to one's self-esteem.

L. J. Sharpe, the author of *The Metropolis Votes*, believes that there is an antagonism between the user, even if he is an academic research worker, and the librarian:

> The non-librarian needs to be comforted and reassured. Who has not seen the reader, when referred to the index, go over to the drawers, hover in confusion, and then sidle off, hoping the assumedly disapproving eye of the librarian is elsewhere?

Speaking of university libraries and undergraduates he says:

> Too often (the undergraduate's) introduction to the library takes the form of a brisk tour through the reading rooms sandwiched between interviews with his tutor . . . and the hundred and one other tasks which crowd the first weeks of his undergraduate life.*

If this is true of undergraduates, then it is much more true for many other men and women, who are not 'introduced' to the library in any way and for whom books are not the tools of their trade.

But why should new members not be asked if they would like to be shown round the library and have it explained to them, if not now, then the next time they come? Some of the earlier quotations show that such

* 'Problems of Social Science information methods from the user's point of view: II. The Research Student', by L. J. Sharpe, in *Information Methods of Research Workers in the Social Sciences*, The Library Association, 1960.

an invitation would not always be accepted: there are people who much prefer to fend for themselves. For them, clear guidance is essential – Luton has a push-button display panel showing where particular subjects are located, like route guides on the Paris Metro. It is a problem for librarians, as for others, that some people welcome personal assistance while others resent it, and this calls for tact from the staff, who must convey that they are approachable if needed.

Part of the solution is suggested by the very fact that many people think of libraries as a kind of shop in which the counter staff are the shop assistants. The comparison may diminish the potentialities of a library and its staff, and yet many libraries could emulate the best run department stores with advantage, in at least three ways.

Large stores employ assistants who act as store guides and do nothing else but tell people where to find what they want. Each guide occupies a prominent position and she may even wear a sash with her function inscribed upon it. She is more approachable than the man or woman who sits at the desk (often rather far into the library) called 'Enquiries', but who usually looks too prepossessed by library business to answer questions.*

The best stores do not expect all of their counter staff to be experts on the merchandise; but they do expect them all to be experts on the referral procedure of the store. They know who in the store has the answer to this customer's question. Libraries could often make better use of their non-professional staff by training them in analogous ways. A barrier is placed between the public and the professional help that they often need, by the insistent equation of librarians in the user's mind with some kind of tally clerk at a turnstile.

Many people, perhaps most people, do not know clearly enough what they want to be able to use a catalogue fruitfully, or even to browse to the best effect. It would help if they could talk more easily to the assistant, if they wished, but talk is generally discouraged by the tomb-like atmosphere that often prevails (and which, as we saw, many users acquiesce in), as though there were no difference in the degree of concentration needed or respect for others called for in the lending departments and the reference room.

Even without an addition to ease of consultation, users would benefit from another device adopted from the store – informative display. Some libraries have learned how to make display encourage the enlargement of

* F. A. Hatt has suggested that reader's advisers or consultants 'should be . . . walking the floor of our public libraries'. The idea is similar in spirit but perhaps too lavish with professional labour. See *Proceedings* of the Public Libraries Conference, pp. 46–47, The Library Association, 1963.

choice, but most make a poor show of it. Display, like librarianship, calls for professional handling. The danger has been vividly foreseen by F. A. Hatt:

> I do hope that one thing we won't be seeing in the public libraries of the 1970s is the old half-imperial sheet covered inexpertly with poster-colour, surrounded by objects borrowed from the puzzled ironmonger down the road and assembled with devilish ingenuity and incongruity, together with a dozen do-it-yourself books.*

'It was just big; I didn't know where to start.' Public libraries, though deficient in many ways, sometimes defeat users with their lavishness. Librarians cannot afford to neglect any device to make choice more feasible, to make the professional knowledge which they possess fully and easily available to the people who need it.

This may be the biggest single transformation that is needed, to enlarge the libraries' effective contact with the public. It is not suggested that librarians should unduly take the initiative, like officious 'can-I-help-you?' salesmen; it is suggested that they are sensitive to whomever needs help in deciding what he wants and where he may find it; and that help should take many forms, not just personal assistance. The degree and the kind of help are indeed two aspects of service that could vary from branch to branch, just as the sophistication and allusiveness of displays could differ according to the nature of the membership. This kind of support from libraries – information readily given, counsel available when sought, reinforced by explicit guiding and informative displays – could strengthen the confidence of the member who, in the end, cannot be bothered to renew his ticket; and it could create a reputation for the library which would enable many of those who remain out of membership to overcome their indifference or diffidence.

Almost everyone agrees that library staffs are pleasant, courteous people. The goodwill is there: it could form the basis of a more creative, less bureaucratic, relationship.

### Libraries are for readers

Much of this is already accepted by many public librarians and yet, even though they want it to be apparent that their libraries are primarily for people, not primarily for storage, there is a distance between them and all but a minority of the public. They are like imperfectly prepared actors who, though they feel emotions of great intensity and turbulence, communicate little to the audience.

This particular study of the audience has shown that libraries do not

* *Proceedings* of the Public Libraries Conference, p. 46.

sufficiently 'project'. (The reasons for this failure are probably complex and would call for a separate study – of librarians and their training, of their relationships with elected committees, of the physical circumstances in which they have to work.) 'Projecting', for an actor, is partly a matter of being audible; of making the gesture large enough to carry; of having the body, the physical equipment, trained to fulfil the player's intentions; and of being helped, not hindered, by acoustics and lighting. For public libraries to demonstrate unequivocably that their attitudes are user-centred, they obviously need to employ the public arts of publicity and promotion with an as yet untried professionalism and seriousness – they need, in short, to be audible; but there are a score of different ways in which libraries could and sometimes do show their user-orientation. They need to make the right gestures, large or small, and these are likely to vary from place to place.

According to local need, libraries would be open at hours when more people might use them, staying open, for instance, until 10 pm on one night a week, or opening on Sunday mornings to relieve the supermarket-like pressure on Saturday. They might install lavatories (as Stepney and Stoke Newington have, and as Chelsea has for children). It would be possible to get into them with a pram (as it is at St Luke's, Finsbury) or have pram parks so that mothers with young children would not have to sever their connection. They would be furnished and lit to create an ambience for browsing. Above all, the arrangement of counters and desks would not be at odds with the spirit and purpose of the enterprise, as they often still are; quite enough is known about library layout for these physical barriers between librarians and their public to be abolished, but many library committees permit obsolete fittings that no progressive store manager would tolerate for a moment.

In a user-centred library service it would not be necessary to argue the case for extension activities (as Harold Jolliffe had to in his comprehensive work on the subject),* nor would it be thought sufficient to justify them because they are a means of drawing attention to a library's main services, especially its bookstock. Yet there are librarians, and probably even more committees, who do not see that the library is the natural centre for lectures, discussion groups, film shows, exhibitions and similar activities as worth-while ends in themselves, and for providing facilities (film and slide projectors, and so on) to enable other agencies in the community to organise such events.

Finally, the examination of the public in the earlier chapters, especially

* *Public Library Extension Activities*, by Harold Jolliffe, The Library Association, 1962.

of the former members, shows that libraries would be able to cater for more people more effectively if they did not take it for granted that people must go to them. There are already three main exceptions to this assumption. The first is the service to local voluntary groups, by providing them with a meeting place or, more important, by lending books and other materials (including sets of plays) that relate to group programmes. Most of the libraries in the seven boroughs lend books to local societies but not all of them do and nor do all their branches. Librarians everywhere should have the time to familiarise themselves with the multiplicity of social, recreative and educative societies in their areas, to know their leaders and to learn about their needs, so that they can lend these groups relevant books, films and other materials; so that they can be more fully, in that telling Americanism, 'resource people'. It is encouraging that this happens already; but it should be more common and the range of groups considered suitable for help should be broadly conceived. Such support ought especially to be available to youth groups; even the least bookish youth club engages in activities to which *some* books are relevant, or with which some film or film strip deals.

The second exception is the service organised for dependent groups in the population. For example, Finsbury Central makes weekly visits to elderly people; Hampstead and Wandsworth have a delivery service to housebound readers and provide deposit collections at houses for the elderly; Stoke Newington also takes books to housebound readers, and Wandsworth lends them to prisoners; Stepney runs the bedside service to patients at one of the local hospitals and five hospitals in Lewisham receive what the librarian described as a 'full service, including talking books and books on microfilm'. Provision of this kind is a start only: it is haphazard (some hospitals are serviced by public libraries, for instance, but others rely on what can be provided by voluntary effort) and a public library that does not undertake this work is not regarded as failing in its duty to the public. Nevertheless, the provision which already exists represents an important and growing attempt to take books to where people are, instead of waiting for people to come to the books. The point at issue, however, is this: there are other ways of being cut off from the resources of public libraries than by being sick, infirm or imprisoned. Part of the solution may be provided by the more liberal and imaginative deployment of deposit collections on fairly short loan wherever people congregate – at work, at leisure, or in church. Another part of the solution is suggested by the third of these extra-mural exceptions.

Mobile libraries are usually used in rural districts where the inhabitants are too scattered to come to a building, or in urban areas to cater for residents on new estates until a permanent library can be built.* But there are educational and spiritual distances to be bridged, not merely geographical ones. Mobile libraries, by circulating with small manageable bookstocks and an assistant to link users with the wider resources of the service, could reinforce the main bases of that service. Obviously mobile libraries cannot meet all needs, but they are not intended to. They would bring books nearer to the diffident, the busy, and even, of course, to the lazy. In so doing, they would enlarge the number of people with the confidence to visit a library; preserve the library habit in people temporarily cut off by looking after small children or settling in to a new house in a new district; and wherever they went, they would publicise the service. This has happened in isolated rural areas; it could also happen in towns. Apart from a diminishing section which is unlikely ever to utilise library facilities, the population splits, at present, into two – those with the qualities to use a public library, and those who have needs that could clearly be met by public libraries but are deterred by character or circumstance from going to them. As long as and wherever these two groups are found in the population, then taking books to people should be as normal as inviting people to the books, and mobile libraries, instead of being a stop gap device, should be a regular extra-mural expression of the libraries' responsibility to the whole public.

At present, public librarians are too often held back by an understandable but limiting concern with the means of professionalism, and not sufficiently with its ends; and by the meanness of their masters. This survey has shown how some people, not only non-members, but people who used to belong and even many of those who still do, are cut off from what their libraries have to offer. The barriers are not wholly of the libraries making, but they are largely so.

To enable libraries to 'project' that they care as much about people as about their books and materials will take imagination (which can wither if it is balked for too long) and money (for more qualified staff and for more adequate stocks). Imaginativeness cannot be laid on; but money can create the conditions for its exercise. In the end, whether public libraries are allowed to continue in their present depressed state (and, compared with the possibilities, this can even be said of some of the London libraries) or whether they will become a many-sided embodiment and nourisher of a literate society's literacy, depends finally not on the standards discussed by the professionals, but on those willed by the public.

* They have also been used in urban areas as a cheap, long-term alternative to branch libraries.

## Table 36 Library stock and expenditure: the seven boroughs

| Borough | Stock (31 March 1963) Adult lending | Refer-ence | Chil-dren | Gramophone records | Expenditure Library rate (d) | Total expenditure (£) |
|---|---|---|---|---|---|---|
| Chelsea | 78,600 | 38,500 | 9,300 | 1,220 | 1.5 | 43,500 |
| Finsbury | 73,400 | 20,600 | 17,400 | 1,800 | 1.8 | 62,000 |
| Hampstead | 170,500 | 38,900 | 28,900 | 8,240 | 3.5 | 108,100 |
| Lewisham | 281,400 | 18,300 | 67,900 | 13,800 | 6.1 | 185,800 |
| Stepney | 125,900 | 14,000 | 26,300 | 5,180 | 2.8 | 79,300 |
| Stoke Newington | 81,100 | 22,800 | 24,600 | 1,590 | 7.8 | 60,800 |
| Wandsworth | 424,300 | 38,600 | 90,800 | 6,840 | 4.1 | 233,600 |

*N.B.*—These figures were supplied by the Association of Metropolitan Chief Librarians.

# The method and the sample, by Jillian MacGuire

The purpose of this appendix is to give a brief account of the sampling procedure and survey method used in the enquiry, the problems encountered and the solutions to them.

Seven boroughs, Chelsea, Finsbury, Hampstead, Lewisham, Stepney, Stoke Newington and Wandsworth, were selected for study, in consultations with the Association of Metropolitan Chief Librarians. A sample of approximately 500 was considered large enough to give a general picture of the relationship between the libraries and their consumers, small enough to permit the full recording of comments, and yet to be within RICA's budget. While it was known that approximately 30 per cent of the population might be expected to be registered library members, no reliable estimate of the relative percentages of former members and non-members could be made. Since RICA was concerned not just with registered members of the public library but with people who had once been registered members and had let their membership lapse, and with people who had never been members at all, it was necessary to draw as representative a sample of the adult population as possible in order to establish the relative proportions of the population falling into the second and third categories.

The use of the electoral register as a sampling frame was rejected for two reasons: it excludes those under 21 years of age; and it excludes people who have recently moved. Since the libraries' adult sections aim to cater for all those who have left school, the age group 15–21 could not be left out of a survey of the relationship between the library and its consumers. It was suspected, with some justification, that moving might be related to the discontinuing of registered membership, so it was important that people who had recently moved should not be excluded. The sample, therefore, would have to be selected 'on the ground' according to a set of instructions designed to make it as random as possible.

Here RICA faced another major problem. If the interviews were carried out with a random sample of 500 the numbers of either former members or non-members interviewed might be too small for any reliable generalisations to be made. If, say, only five per cent of the population had never been members then only about 50 interviews with non-members would take place, and this was felt to be too small a number for any further breakdown in terms of age, sex, occupation, intelligence or any other variables in which the enquiry would be interested.

Consequently it was decided to draw an equal number of respondents from each borough and an equal number of members, former members and non-members, representative in terms of sex and occupational status of the total population of the seven boroughs. In order to select such a sample more than 500 people would need to be contacted. If this larger group were contacted on a random basis, they would give an estimate of the distribution of members, former members and non-members in the total population.

The sample to be interviewed was to be stratified in accordance with the following profile:

| | Occupied | | | Non-occupied | | |
|---|---|---|---|---|---|---|
| | Members | Former members | Non-members | Members | Former members | Non-members |
| Male | 70 | 70 | 70 | 7 | 7 | 7 |
| Female | 35 | 35 | 35 | 56 | 56 | 56 |
| Totals | 105 | 105 | 105 | 63 | 63 | 63 |

The total sample to be interviewed was 504. Forty-five per cent of the sample was to be male and 55 per cent female to be representative of the male/female ratio in the boroughs at the 1951 Census, i.e. 231 were therefore to be male and 273 to be female. Ninety per cent of the men (210) were to be occupied and 40 per cent of the women (105), to be representative of the population.

The random sample of contacts was selected 'on the ground' by the interviewers according to prepared instructions. The sites of the libraries were plotted on a map of each of the seven boroughs. Certain libraries, selected so as to give maximum geographical coverage of the areas, were taken as starting-points for interviewers. Routes from the library were marked on the map and interviewers were instructed to call on houses at regular intervals along these routes. The following instructions were given:

> Follow the prescribed route(s) from each public library. In high density areas the sampling interval is every tenth rateable unit; in low density areas every fifth. Exception: blocks of flats. Take one per floor and/or per staircase in strict sequence, e.g. staircase (or floor) one, flats 1–20, call at flat 1; staircase two, flats 21–30, call at flat 22; staircase three, flats 31–40, call at flat 33.

*N.B.*—Houses converted into flats. Treat the house as a calling unit, but select bell in sequence, e.g. flat 1 at first conversion, flat 2 at second, etc.

Call back policy: three attempts should be made to get an interview at the selected unit.

Interviewers were instructed to cover evening periods as well as the morning and afternoon, so that the working population, shift workers and men, had an equal chance of inclusion and so that the final sample should not be overweighted with housewives at home all day. Transitory visitors, not normally living at the address called at, were excluded.

Interviewers were given special 'contact sheets' on which to record details about the relationship to the library of all those contacted, their sex, estimated age and their occupational status. The interviewers were instructed to select for a full interview those contacts who matched their quota in terms of age, occupation, sex and relationship to the library. Different questions were to be asked of members, former members and non-members; these were tested in the pilot surveys and the final questionnaire (Appendix 3) was divided into three distinct sections to make interviewing and tabulation more simple.

In the field it soon became obvious from interviewers' reports that it was going to be practically impossible to achieve a rectangular sub-sample of members, former members and non-members, although this problem had not appeared at the pilot stage. Only 239 of the quota were yielded by 661 contacts. Interviewers were finding difficulty in completing parts of their quotas. One interviewer in Stoke Newington, for instance, reckoned that it would take her 200 calls to find the seven male occupied former members she needed to complete her quota. A compromise was decided on whereby an attempt should be made to complete 168 interviews with members leaving the remaining 336 interviews to be completed as soon as practicable with former members and non-members. The final sub-sample of completed interviews was 501, a slightly awkward total. The three segments of the sub-sample were, in the end, neither equal in size nor representative of the population contacted in proportion to their relation to the public library service. The members interviewed can, however, be taken as representing the total contacted population. Thirty per cent of the contacts were registered members and 32 per cent of the interviewed sample were registered members. This difference was not significant. Similarly all non-members can be taken as representative but within this group former members are over-represented in comparison with the proportion of former members among the contacts.

In total 1,306 people were contacted (the first stage) in the course of the enquiry to yield the 501 (the second stage) who were interviewed in detail about their relationship to the public library. How representative were these 1,306 (first stage) contacts of the population in the seven boroughs?

Women were considerably over-represented among the total contacted. Sixty-five per cent of the 1,306 who answered the questions on the contact sheet were women and 35 per cent were men.

Table A Library use by sex

| | Male | | Female | | Total* | |
|---|---|---|---|---|---|---|
| Total contacted | Number | Per cent | Number | Per cent | Number | Per cent |
| Members | 152 | 33 | 244 | 29 | 396 | 30 |
| Former members | 117 | 26 | 200 | 23 | 317 | 24 |
| Non-members | 186 | 41 | 407 | 48 | 593 | 46 |

* Total contacted 1,306.

| | Male | | Female | | Total† | |
|---|---|---|---|---|---|---|
| Sample interviewed | Number | Per cent | Number | Per cent | Number | Per cent |
| Members | 85 | 37 | 75 | 28 | 160 | 32 |
| Former members | 65 | 28 | 79 | 29 | 144 | 29 |
| Non-members | 81 | 35 | 116 | 43 | 197 | 39 |

† Sample interviewed 501.

The difference between the male and female patterns of library use on the basis of the total sample contacted was not significant even at the ten per cent level ($\chi^2=3 \cdot 79$, df=2, $P>0 \cdot 10$). Women are not significantly less likely than men to be registered members, nor are they significantly more likely than men to be non-members. Although the contacted sample is overweighted with women the percentages of registered members, former members and non-members are not significantly affected by this overweighting.

To what extent can the 501 (second stage) people interviewed be regarded as representative of the population in the seven boroughs in terms of sex, age, terminal education ages and occupation?

**Sex**

It was important that the sample should not be overweighted with women at home, a danger which always faces an 'on the ground' sample selection procedure. The quotas of male and female respondents were therefore laid down on the basis of the 1951 Census Report for the seven boroughs taken as a whole, and the sample actually achieved was exactly comparable with the percentage distribution in the seven boroughs at the time of the 1951 Census.

Table B Sex of sample compared with the population of the seven boroughs aged 15 and over (1961 Census figures)

| | Borough population | | Sample | |
|---|---|---|---|---|
| | Totals | Per cent | Totals | Per cent |
| Male | 330,983 | 46 | 231 | 46 |
| Female | 378,025 | 54 | 270 | 54 |

Forty-six per cent of the over 15 population in the seven boroughs was male and 54 per cent female at the time of the 1961 Census. The following table (Table C) shows the sex distribution of the people interviewed in the survey in 1962, according to their relationship to the library:

Table C The sample: number, sex, library relationship

| | Library use | | | Number | Per cent |
|---|---|---|---|---|---|
| | Members | Former | Never | interviewed | distribution |
| Male | 85 | 65 | 81 | 231 | 46 |
| Female | 75 | 79 | 116 | 270 | 54 |
| Total | 160 | 144 | 197 | 501 | 100 |

The overall sample is therefore representative in terms of sex ratio. Women are slightly under-represented among members and over-represented among non-members. The differences in sex ratio between the three sub-samples are not significant at the five per cent level ($\chi^2=5\cdot12$ df$=2$ $0\cdot10>P>0\cdot50$). Though these differences exist they are not quite large enough to justify the assertion that men are more likely to be registered members than women.

## Age

The County of London Report on the 1961 Census gives the latest available information on the age structure of the seven boroughs. At the time of coding the data it was not thought that the 1961 Census data would be available for comparison and slightly different groupings from the Census were used. This makes the comparison between the two sets of data rather less valuable from the point of view of assessing the representativeness of the survey sample.

In fact the library sample compares very closely with the Census distribution. The former is slightly overweighted in the 21–35 age group and underweighted in the 66+ age group. The sample can justifiably be

Table D Age: the sample compared with 1961 Census figures

| | | 15–19 | 20–34 | 35–54 | 55–64 | 65+ | Total |
|---|---|---|---|---|---|---|---|
| Census 1961 | Number | 60 | 189 | 255 | 104 | 110 | 709* |
| | Per cent | 8 | 25 | 36 | 15 | 16 | 100 |

* Number correct to the nearest thousand.

| | | 15–20 | 21–35 | 36–55 | 56–65 | 66+ | Total |
|---|---|---|---|---|---|---|---|
| Library sample | Number | 37 | 145 | 181 | 70 | 61 | 494 |
| | Per cent | 8 | 30 | 36 | 14 | 12 | 100* |

* Seven people gave no information.

regarded as reasonably representative of the age structure of the total adult population of the seven boroughs.

**Terminal education age**

The 1961 Census Report for the County of London does not contain any information on the age at which the inhabitants of the London boroughs completed their full-time education. The County Report on the 1951 Census does give information on terminal education ages for the occupied population, but not for the total population. Since 1951 the age at which people complete their education has tended to rise and it might be expected that the higher terminal age categories in a sample drawn in 1962 would be proportionately larger. The RICA sample, however, included the non-occupied as well as the occupied population, which might be expected to have had fewer years of education than the occupied population. Table E shows that the library sample was not markedly different in trend from the Census distribution, though people completing their education at 16 would seem to be slightly under-represented.

Table E Terminal education age: the sample compared with the Census

| | | Under 15 | 15 | 16 | 17–19 | Over 20 | Total |
|---|---|---|---|---|---|---|---|
| 1951 Census | Number | 159 | 54 | 47 | 42 | 17 | 319* |
| | Per cent | 50 | 17 | 15 | 13 | 5 | 100 |
| Survey sample | Number | 265 | 78 | 40 | 59 | 45 | 487† |
| | Per cent | 54 | 16 | 8 | 13 | 9 | 100 |

* Numbers correct to the nearest thousand.
† Nine people were still in full-time education, three had not been educated, two gave no information.

The value of this comparison is somewhat limited but it does show that the RICA sample is not heavily overweighted with highly educated respondents and that those who completed their education at the minimum possible age are fully represented.

## Occupation

The occupations of the sample of 501 were classified on the basis of the occupational index used by BBC Audience Research. This was chosen in preference to the Registrar-General's classification on two grounds: the proportions of the population fall into each category more evenly than the proportions falling into the Registrar-General's five classes; secondly, the the BBC index is more closely related to education, intelligence and the degree of responsibility of a given occupational status. Unfortunately there is no regional breakdown for the London area against which the distribution of the survey sample can be checked. The following table (Table F) shows the distribution of a 7,000 national sample drawn in 1963 by the BBC (and not hitherto published) and puts the distribution of the library sample alongside for comparison.

Table F Occupations of sample compared with the BBC's national sample

| Classification | BBC national sample Per cent | Survey sample Number | Survey sample Per cent |
|---|---|---|---|
| 1 Professional | 7 (1–2 combined) | 35 | 7 |
| 2 Managerial | | 30 | 6 |
| 3 Lower managerial and executive | 10 | 96 | 19 |
| 4 Highly skilled and senior clerical | 25 | 85 | 17 |
| 5 Skilled and lower clerical | 20 | 93 | 18 |
| 6 Semi-skilled | 18 | 69 | 14 |
| 7 Unskilled | 12 | 54 | 11 |
| Unclassifiable | 8 | 39 | 8 |
| | 100 | 501 | 100 |

In comparison with the national sample the survey sample is overweighted with people in professional and managerial occupations. It is not possible to say for certain whether this weighting is due to the sample being unrepresentative or whether the library sample accurately reflects the seven boroughs' atypical occupational profile. London, as a whole, differs in occupational composition from the nation, and since the capital has more than its fair share of professional personnel it is not surprising that the sample drawn from the seven boroughs should not exactly match the national sample.

# The Questionnaire

Before using the questionnaire, interviewers introduced themselves and recorded certain details about everyone with whom they made contact – sex, whether (ever) a member of a public library, whether occupied or not, etc. Contacts that met quota requirements were then taken on to the questionnaire proper. This Appendix reproduces its content but not the format or layout; the phrases used in several questions, though summarised on the schedule, were spoken in full by the interviewers. For example, for Question 3, Item E (study/homework), they said, '. . . has a room for studying or for children to do homework?' The cards displayed in Question 9 and 18 also used complete statements. 'Y/N/DK' represent 'yes, no and don't know.'

1. How long have you lived in........................ (name borough)?
   - Temporary
   - New to district
   - Not new (over 12 months)

2. Can you tell me where the nearest public library is?
   - Definitely knows
   - Knows vaguely
   - Does not know

   Is that the central or a branch library?
   - Knows
   - Does not know

   Can you also tell me where the nearest cinema is?

3. To help us find out whether the local library's publicity is good enough, would you mind telling us whether your library (has a) (prompt)
   - A. Children's library Y/N/DK
   - B. Lends records Y/N/DK
   - C. Reading room with MS. Y/N/DK
   - D. Public lectures Y/N/DK
   - E. Study/homework Y/N/DK
   - F. All kinds of information Y/N/DK

4. Do you know whether you can use public libraries in other boroughs, where you work, for example?
   - Can/Not/DK

5. Do you happen to belong to a library other than the public one? — No
   (If yes) which one is that? — University/College; Specialist/London library; Subscription; Other
   (If yes) why do you belong to it?

---

(Former members go on to Question 13, members to Question 23. Ask NON-MEMBERS only Questions 6–11)

---

6. Do you read books borrowed from the public library by other members of the household? (If necessary) I mean books not magazines. — No; Yes

7. (*a*) Everyone is entitled to *use* public libraries, even if they're not members. Do you use it at all? (Prompt) For example, reading newspapers/magazines there? Or do you ever use or work in the reference library? — Does not use; Reading/Reference/Other
   (*b*) (If some non-registered use) About how often do you go there? — Uses at least weekly; monthly; intermittently
   (*c*) (If some non-registered use) (Probe) Can you tell me more about the kind of use you make of the...........................................?

8. In fact many people are like yourself, they don't belong to public libraries, even though we all pay for them. Why do you suppose this is? (Record spontaneous reply)
   Would these be your reasons too? (Record reply) — Partly yes/Yes/No

9. Here are other reasons which people sometimes give. Do you think any of these are good reasons? (Show card – rotate) (Probe throughout) — Books dirty/unhygienic; Librarians starchy; Building grim; Can't get right books; Reading? Not interested; Travelling costly, etc.; It costs too much

10. Have you ever, as a matter of interest, been inside the local library to see what it is like? (If yes) what did you think about it? (Record comment) — Not inside/Inside

11. Do you think you might ever want to use it? — Might use/Not

---

(Ask FORMER MEMBERS only Questions 12–22)

---

| | |
|---|---|
| 12. Which public library used you to belong to? (Specify) | ...................... Can't remember |
| How long ago was that (roughly)? | Within 12 months<br>1–3 years ago<br>4–10 years ago<br>Longer ago<br>Can't remember |
| 13. What kind of use did you make of it? (Prompt) Did you | Borrow books?<br>Borrow Records?<br>Read newspapers, etc.?<br>Look things up in ref. room?<br>Other? |
| 14. Roughly how often did you use it? (Running prompt) | Nearly every week<br>About once a month<br>Say every 3 months<br>Less often<br>Intermittently |
| 15. Do you read books borrowed from the public library by other members of the household? | No<br>Yes |
| 16. (*a*) Everyone is entitled to *use* the public library, even if they're not members. Do you use it at all? (Prompt) For example, reading newspapers/magazines there? Or do you ever use/work in the reference library? | Does not<br>Reading/Reference/Other |
| (*b*) (If some non-registered use) About how often do you do that? | Use at least weekly<br>monthly<br>intermittently |
| (*c*) (If some non-registered use) (Probe) Can you tell me more about the kind of use you make of the..........................................? | |
| 17. Can you recall why you gave up belonging to the library? | |
| 18. Here are other reasons that people sometimes give. Are any of these something like your own reasons? (Show card – rotate) (Probe throughout) | Moved – broke habit<br>Gave up studying<br>Preferred other activities<br>Prefer to buy books<br>Could not get books wanted<br>Inconvenient hours<br>Eyesight, other handicap<br>Unpleasant atmosphere<br>Unpleasant staff<br>Rules/Fines nuisance<br>Travelling costly, etc.<br>Gave it up – marriage, etc. |

| | |
|---|---|
| 19. (*a*) Is there some service you think the local library should offer but doesn't? (Probe) (Record suggestions) | No/DK/Yes |
| (*b*) If the library laid this on, would you consider joining/using it again? | Yes/No/DK |
| 20. Have you been inside the local library recently? (If yes) what did you think about it? (Record comment) | Not inside/Inside |
| 21. Do you think you might ever use it? | Might use/Not |
| 22. Why do you suppose more people don't use the public library service? (Record reply) | |

---

(Ask MEMBERS only Questions 23–36)

---

| | |
|---|---|
| 23. Which public library(ies) do you use? (Record answers) (If both, restrict subsequent answers to local library) | Local/Elsewhere/Both |
| 24. What kind of use do you make of the library? (Prompt) Do you | Borrow books?<br>Borrow records?<br>Use reading room?<br>Use reference library?<br>Other? |
| 25. About how often do you go to the library? (Running prompt) (If someone else goes on respondent's behalf, ring two positions) | At least weekly<br>About once a fortnight<br>Say once a month<br>Once in 3 months<br>Less often<br>Intermittently<br>Someone else goes |
| 26. (*a*) Do you find it easy to get the kind of books you want? (Probe) | Yes/Fairly/No |
| (*b*) (If relevant) Do you find it easy to get the type of records you want? (Probe) | Yes/Fairly/No |
| (*c*) (If relevant) Do you find it easy to get the kind of reference information you want? (Probe) | Yes/Fairly/No |
| 27. What is your general impression of the staff? (Running prompt) (Probe) | Very good/Good/Adequate/ Fair/Poor |
| 28. (*a*) Would you say that the library's outside appearance was attractive or off-putting? (Probe) | Satis./So-so/Unsatis. |
| (*b*) What about the appearance and layout inside? (Probe) | Satis./So-so/Unsatis. |
| (*c*) What about the lighting? | Well-lit/Adequate/Poor |
| (*d*) And the furniture? | Satis./So-so/Unsatis. |

29. Are you satisfied with the:

| | |
|---|---|
| system for returning books? | Y/N/DK |
| cataloguing system? | Y/N/DK |
| renewal system? | Y/N/DK |

(If no, probe)

| | |
|---|---|
| 30. Can you reserve books in your library? | Y/N/DK |
| (If yes) Have you ever tried to reserve a book? (Record whether frequently or rarely) | Y/N |
| (If yes) Did/does it work satisfactorily? (Probe) | Satis./So-so/Unsatis. |

| | |
|---|---|
| 31. Can your library borrow books for you from other libraries? | Y/N/DK |
| (If yes) Have you ever asked them to? (Record frequency) | Y/N |
| (If yes) Did/does the system work satisfactorily? (Probe) | Satis./So-so/Unsatis. |

| | |
|---|---|
| 32. Do you think that the rules and regulations are (prompt) (Probe, if negative) | Reasonable?<br>Acceptable?<br>Unreasonable?<br>DK |

33. What do you think about fines? (Probe)

| | |
|---|---|
| 34. Do other people in the household read books which you borrow from the public library? | Y/N |
| (If yes) Are they members too? | Y/N/Both |

| | | |
|---|---|---|
| 35. How well do you think these other public services are doing their job on the whole? (Running prompt) | Refuse Collection | E/G/A<br>F/P /DK |
| | Electricity Board | E/G/A<br>F/P /DK |
| | Income Tax | E/G/A<br>F/P /DK |
| | London Transport | E/G/A<br>F/P /DK |
| | and the Public Libraries? | E/G/A<br>F/P /DK |

36. Why do you suppose more people don't use the public library service?

---

(Ask ALL Questions 37–40)

---

| | |
|---|---|
| 37. How many books of your own do you have, roughly? | 0/1–50/50–100/100–200<br>200–500/500+ |

38. (*a*) Did your school try to encourage you to become a public library user? — N/DK

(*b*) (If yes) What kind of encouragement? (Prompt if necessary) — School library / Public library visits / Influence of teachers / General

(*c*) (Do *not* ask non-members.) (If no) Do you remember how you first came to be a public library user?

39. How do you look back on your schooldays, *on the whole*? Which of these statements comes closest to your own feelings? They are about whether you *liked* being at school or not, not about whether you think you learned much! (Show card and read out)
A. I liked them very much
B. I liked them quite a bit
C. They were all right, but nothing special
D. I didn't like them much
E. I disliked them very much

40. And which one of these, which are about whether you think you learned much? (Show card)
A. I learned a great deal that was useful to me
B. I learned quite a bit
C. School was all right, but nothing special
D. They didn't teach me all that much
E. They taught me hardly anything

## CLASSIFICATION AND ASSESSMENT

41. Male member/former member/non-member (male) — M/FM/NM
Female member/former member/non-member (female) — M/FM/NM

42. Education (last full-time schooling only)
University
Teacher training, etc.
Technical college
Private college (Pitman's etc.)
Public school
County High/Grammar
Technical school
Private school
Central/Sec. Mod.
Elem./Church
Other

43. Age left school (complete full-time education)

44. Occupation (former main, if retired)
    Industry
    No. of staff controlled (if any)
    (If housewife)
        Former occupation (if any)
        Industry
        No. of staff
    (If housewife, if any husband)
        Husband's occupation
        Industry
        No. of staff

45. Age last birthday

46. Evaluation of respondent's attitude

| | | |
|---|---|---|
| Interested | Co-operative | Sincere |
| Indifferent | Amenable | Evasive |
| Uninterested | Hostile | Unreliable |

47. Address of interview: Borough
    Distance

- - - - - - - - - - - - - - - - - - - - - - - - - - - - - - - - - - - - - - - - - - - - -

48. Interviewer's name: Date of interview:

- - - - - - - - - - - - - - - - - - - - - - - - - - - - - - - - - - - - - - - - - - - - -

# Selected reading list


**Official reports, etc.**

*Inter-library Co-operation in England and Wales* HMSO, 1962.
*Public Libraries and Museums Bill*, 67/1964 HMSO, 1964.
*Standards of Public Library Service in England and Wales* HMSO, 1962.
*Standards of Reading 1948–56* Ministry of Education, HMSO, 1957.
*The Structure of the Public Library Service in England and Wales:* report of the Committee appointed by the Minister of Education in September 1957 HMSO, 1959 (Cmnd. 660).

**Books and pamphlets**

*The Chance to Read: public libraries in the world today* Lionel R. McColvin Phoenix House, 1956.

*The Communication of ideas* T. Cauter and J. S. Downham Chatto and Windus for *Reader's Digest*, 1954.

*Education and Retirement* Brian Groombridge National Institute of Adult Education, 1960.

*Gramophone Record Libraries* Ed. H. F. J. Currall Crosby Lockwood, 1963.

*Libraries: Free-for-All?* A. P. Herbert Institute of Economic Affairs, 1962.

*Libraries in Scandinavia* K. C. Harrison Deutsch, 1961.

*The Library's Public* B. Berelson Columbia University Press (New York), 1949.

*The Metropolis Votes* L. J. Sharpe Greater London Papers, No. 8, London School of Economics, 1962.

*Penny Rate: aspects of British Public Library History, 1850–1950*
W. A. Munford The Library Association, 1951.

*Public Libraries Today* K. C. Harrison Crosby Lockwood, 1963.

*The Public Library: its origins, purposes and significance as a social institution* W. J. Murison Harrap, 1955.

*Public Library Extension Activities* Harold Jolliffe The Library Association, 1962.

*The Public Library System of Great Britain: a report on its present condition with proposals for post-war reorganisation* Lionel R. McColvin The Library Association, 1942.

*Reading in Tottenham* Borough of Tottenham, Libraries and Museum Department, 1947.

**Other publications**

*Book Provision for Special Needs* The Library Association (London and Home Counties Branch), 1962.

'Books in London, 1959', *Books*, Journal of National Book League, January–February 1960.

*The Library Association Record*, published monthly.

*The London Librarian*, London and Home Counties Branch, published monthly.

*Proceedings of the Conference of The Library Association*, published annually.

# Index

The heading 'Libraries' has been used to signify 'Public libraries'.

A number followed by *n* indicates a footnote.

The 'List of Tables' should also be consulted.